STA
INVESTING

STEPHEN R. DATZ

GENERAL PHILATELIC CORPORATION
LOVELAND, COLORADO

PRINTING HISTORY
First printing: December 1997
Second printing: December 1999
Third printing: September 2003

ISBN: 0-88219-029-6

Cover design: Mike Jenson

Manufactured in the United States of America

Published by General Philatelic Corporation
Division of General Trade Corporation
Post Office Box 402
Loveland, Colorado 80539

Philatelic Books by Stephen R. Datz

ACKNOWLEDGMENTS

My sincere thanks to John Hotchner for generously taking the time to work with the manuscript and offer suggestions and criticisms, which were immensely helpful. Thanks to Judy Waller for proofreading. Thanks to my wife, Susan, for proofreading and suggestions, but most of all for her patience during preparation of this book and during all our years in business. And thanks are due all the buyers and sellers of stamps who, over the years, provided me with the experiences that are the basis for the insights presented in this book.

CONTENTS

FOREWORD

This book arose in response to questions frequently asked by collectors and others interested in stamps as investments. It is not a tout book as were most of the stamp investment books written during the Great Boom of the late 1970s, which treated stamps as foolproof investments with unlimited upside and no downside. If only it were true! Sadly, it is not.

During the years following the great boom, countless mass-marketed stamp investment portfolios came through my door. They looked strikingly similar, plush binders containing mint stamps mounted in clear plastic mounts on printed pages. The stamps, too, looked strikingly similar—an endless procession of $5 Coolidges and $5 Hamiltons, 50-cent "baby" Zeppelins, sets of Lexington-Concord commemoratives, and the like.

Almost without exception, sellers reacted with disappointment and amazement when told what their portfolios were worth and almost without exception lamented, "But I thought stamps were supposed to be a good investment!"

I could only answer that some were, but many were not. At the same time, I noticed that other investors had done remarkably well. As time passed, I began to think about who had made money in stamps and who had not. I realized that those who had been successful invariably had taken the time and trouble to become knowledgeable and experienced. It made all the difference.

This book will try to approach stamps dispassionately, the same way seasoned investors approach any other potential investment.

It will endeavor to be realistic, objective and disciplined. It will not naively subscribe to the hollow notion that all stamps possess magical investment value.

It will touch on economic history, the economy in general and the economics of the stamp trade in specific to give you insight into what makes stamp prices rise and fall. This because investing in stamps—and investing in general—is like flying the Alaskan bush—you'd better know the terrain or you're going to find yourself in trouble.

Glossy investment pamphlets loaded with slick graphics and glib promises won't cut it. My experience has been that those who rely on others to make them money usually come away disappointed. They buy the wrong stamps at the wrong time for the wrong reasons. The truth is, you have to do your own homework. And that's what this book will emphasize. Your success will be proportional to the amount of time you spend becoming knowledgeable about stamps and the stamp market.

Hopefully, you'll come away with a frame of reference against which to measure opportunities. As I've said, you won't find recommendations for specific items in this book, but rather an emphasis on knowledge, strategy, and tactics. The idea is to learn how to recognize potentially profitable situations and how to avoid those that are not. In other words, how to call your own shots.

Is stamp investment for everyone? No. There's the matter of temperament and of expectation. Investors usually do best in areas they have intuition for. It's no different with stamps. Ironically, it is often the meticulously formed specialized collection—the collection formed without regard to future value—that turns out to yield the best return.

A bit about my background. My formal training is in economics. I became a full-time stamp dealer in the early 1970s. In the course of my career, I've bought and sold thousands of collections. And I've seen innumerable stamp investment services come and go. While the market was hot, they sprouted like the wildflowers that dot the meadow beyond my study window each spring—and most turned out to be as ephemeral.

There are those who will be annoyed with me for what I have to say in this book—especially since it does not promote some of the cardinal myths of stamp investment—but the stamp business has been good to me, and I feel that I owe it to readers and to the hobby to tell things as I see them.

Unlike the tout books, the purpose of this book is to tell you about stamps as investments, not sell you on the idea of investing in stamps. If you enjoy stamps, there's no reason why you shouldn't profit from them as well. When you have finished reading, you can decide for yourself if stamps make sense to you as investments. If you decide they do, you'll have the benefit of some realistic insights.

THE GREAT BOOM

During the decade of the 1970s, stamp prices increased tenfold. The stamp market boomed with the raw energy of a nineteenth century gold camp. The rush was on, and those who were there remember the Great Boom as the high point in the stamp market.

Making money was as easy as buying stamps. And if you guessed wrong and paid too much, the market bailed you out in short order, often in a matter of weeks. Collectors and dealers eagerly awaited each new edition of the *Scott Catalogue* and the *Brookman Catalogue* to see how much their holdings had risen in price. Everything was going up and there seemed no end to it.

Buy ads in philatelic weeklies begged for stamps, offered to pay 80 percent, 90 percent, 100 percent, even as much as 120 percent of catalogue for better stamps. Prices rose so quickly that catalogue makers couldn't keep up with them. Some began factoring in price increases, guessing where the market would be at publication time weeks or months in the future.

Dealers—myself included—couldn't keep stamps in stock. Inventory went out the door as fast as it came in, and customers weren't particularly price conscious—they just wanted stamps. The problem wasn't selling, but how to replace inventory. We bought everything we could lay our hands on at whatever price it took because we knew that if we waited, it would only cost more later.

As prices continued to rise, collectors became less inclined to part with stamps. They were as good as gold—better, in fact. The only way to pry stamps out of the woodwork was to offer higher and higher prices, which only put more pressure on the market and caused prices to rise even further. By the late 1970s the whirlwind of buying had turned into a hurricane of speculation.

At the time, double-digit inflation and the lurking threat of hyperinflation withered the performance of stocks and bonds. Financial assets were in the dumps. Everyone wanted tangible assets and, among them, stamps were being touted as *the* fool-proof investment. Even the broader world seemed to be taking notice. In 1978, Salomon Brothers, the prestigious Wall Street investment firm, included stamps in its survey of comparative investment performance. Stamps, it seemed, were now in the big leagues, right along with stocks, bonds, foreign exchange, housing, diamonds and oil. It was as if the world had suddenly discovered what collectors had known all along—stamps were great investments. According to the 1979 Salomon Brothers survey, stamps rose 60.9 percent during the preceding 12 months compared with 5.3 percent for stocks and 3.3 percent for bonds. Stamps outstripped the rate of inflation, which was 10.5 percent, by nearly a factor of five.

Stamp investment firms sprang up like weeds. They touted the virtues of stamps as investments with slick brochures featuring full-color photos of rarities, graphs of precipitous gains, and serious-looking fellows in three-piece suits. Together with a spate of stamp investment books, they hammered home what were considered to be the Great Truths of stamp investment, which were that stamps (1) had increased in value steadily since day one; (2) had never lost value, and were, in fact, one of the few assets that did not decline in value during the Great Depression; and (3), historically, had increased in value at a rate significantly greater than that of inflation. In addition, stamps were portable, invisible (not registered), highly liquid (all over the world, it was said), and generated no current taxable income. Stamps were the perfect investment—unlimited upside *and no downside!*

Dealers cited the Great Truths and the Salomon Brothers figures with evangelic fervor—and innocently it must be noted, for they too were believers.

The number of people calling themselves stamp dealers burgeoned, as did the number of stamp investment services. Most of the stamp investment services had not been regular stamp dealers before the boom, and most would vanish once the bubble burst.   Customers who had spent only $25 or $50 at a time suddenly began spending hundreds, even thousands of dollars on stamps.

"Is it a good investment?" buyers invariably asked.

"Absolutely," dealers invariably answered, citing the Great Truths and the Salomon Brothers' figures.   And no matter what their advice, the market proved them right.   Before long, stamp dealers began to look like investment wizards, and perhaps got an exaggerated sense of their own knowledge.   Everyone, it seemed, wanted their advice, and while expert in things philatelic, few had any formal training or experience in things financial.   They usually answered questions about investment-worthiness in terms of philatelic attributes—grade, scarcity, desirability—rather than in terms of financial merit, risk, liquidity, or economics.   But no one noticed or cared.   Stamp prices were rising fast and everyone wanted in on the action.

Mass marketers began selling investment portfolios by direct mail.   They offered plans for every budget—$100, $500, $1,000 per month, or more.   Sales boomed.   Promoters weren't too concerned about what they had to pay to get "investment grade" stock, which finally came to mean just about any mint, never-hinged stamp free of faults worth $10 or more.   They paid whatever it took, marked it up accordingly, and passed the cost on to clients.

The stamp market was awash with money.   Stamps sold themselves.   Collectors found themselves having to elbow their way to bourse tables, hoping something desirable might be left to buy.   Everybody bought.   Everybody made money.   Everybody was happy.   Dealers ate caviar and drank champagne.   It was a season of universal euphoria, the likes of which the hobby had never seen before.

In the final months of the frenzy, it was possible to walk a show floor, buy a lot for $5,000 (or whatever figure) and sell it elsewhere on the floor for a ten percent (or greater) profit.   Some dealers made thousands simply working the floor with no inventory other than what they bought and sold.   The hurricane of speculation roared ahead gathering more and more energy from the warm sea of optimism. It swept up everyone in its path.

Then in 1980, it made landfall, moved onto the terrain that would later be known as the Reagan years, and on this new terrain, it quickly lost energy and dissipated.

Buyers disappeared as rapidly as they had appeared. Prices fell. Dealers dropped like flies. The market lay in shambles. By the mid-1980s, the market had lost 60 percent to 70 percent of its value. The U.S. Zeppelin set of 1930, which had traded for as much as $8,000 in superb condition during the height of the boom, could now be had for $2,500. The Great Truths lay shattered, revealed to be Great Myths. The grand and glorious party was over, and the stamp market would never be the same again.

During the early 1980s, catalogue publishers adjusted prices downward only slightly, hedging against the possibility that the market might turn and catch them flat footed. Everyone wanted to believe that the market would rebound. It was just a matter of time, they reasoned. The expectation continued even into the mid-1980s. Catalogue prices continued to remain artificially high and the market grew accustomed to trading in discounts of catalogue, which at least offered the illusion that bargains were to be had. By 1988, it was not unusual to see mint foreign stamps retailing for as little as 25 percent to 33 percent of catalogue, and dealers got used to paying 10 percent to 20 percent of catalogue for stamps.

The market did not rebound and in 1988, the *Scott Catalogue* lowered catalogue prices to more closely conform to actual retail prices. In many cases the reductions were severe. The sudden, drastic drop in catalogue prices shocked the market, yet at the same time provided the final dramatic acknowledgement that the Great Boom was over—and would not return anytime soon.

After 1980, when the market began to unravel, one increasingly heard the comment that greedy investors had ruined the market and that it was good to see them gone. In addition, many opined, somewhat self-righteously, that losing money served investors right, that they got exactly what they deserved. And now, the self-righteous harrumphed, the market could be reclaimed by those to whom it rightly belonged—collectors.

Who were these mysterious investors, anyway?   Had they ruined the market?   What caused the Great Boom?   How had stamps come through the depression unscathed only to take a beating in the 1980s?   When would the market recover?   Would stamps boom again?   Are stamps good investments?   Can you really make money with them?

That's what this book is all about.

WHO WERE THE INVESTORS

During and shortly after the boom of the late 1970s, one heard much complaining from collectors that investors had taken over the market and ruined it. Their tone of voice implied that investors were low-life, money-grubbing scum. But who were these mysterious, elusive investors?

During the Great Boom, I met with Wall Street money men, pension plan managers, trust officers, and innumerable tangibles seminar attendees to discuss stamps as investments. During that time, I never met a single investor who was not first a stamp collector or at least interested in stamps. Not one. Those who were not interested in stamps as investments, without exception, had no experience with stamps or any interest in knowing more about them.

At the same time, most—if not all—collectors were buying stamps hand over fist. They couldn't seem to get enough.
Some were rich, but most were solidly middle-class. They had worked hard for their money and were just eager to participate in the good fortune of the hobby. They bought—even overbought—rationalizing that their expenditures would rise in value. They had become investors.

Dealers, too, jumped in with both feet. They bought heavily, conscious of rising replacement costs. And their enthusiasm rubbed off on their customers. Material disappeared from the market, which only fueled the speculation.

The evil, greedy investors were not outside opportunists who suddenly swooped down on the market, drained it of stamps, reaped obscene profits, then left collectors holding the bag and in the process, ruined the market. No, it was those who enjoyed stamps who fueled the boom. It was the Dr. Jekyll collector whose shift from collecting to speculating created the Mr. Hyde investor.

Nor did dealers ruin the market as some have suggested. They simply participated in the feeding frenzy like everyone else, and perhaps suffered more when the party was over. More than half the dealers who had been operating during the boom went under in the early 1980s, most with losses. Almost none would ever return. As prices softened, they found themselves loaded with expensive inventory that they could liquidate only at a loss. Those with the most debt suffered early and went down first.

There was no corresponding rush to sell among collectors, who typically hold onto their stamps until they decide to quit collecting anyway. At least they had their stamps, unlike the dealers who had gone belly-up. They just held on as prices slipped.

Collectors want their stamps to appreciate over time and that requires a healthy, optimistic market. Stamp investors are part of a healthy vibrant market. Dealers have to be successful in order to be able to continue to buy stamps and stock those that collectors demand. Ironically, the larger the number of successful dealers, the more vigorous the market. The more vigorous the market, the better potential for prices to rise. Even speculators have a place. Those who hoarded new issues during the decades following the 1930s are responsible for those stamps remaining affordably priced to this day. So although they did not make a profit, they made a contribution to the hobby by providing the broad range of inexpensive stamps that entry-level collectors enjoy today.

Yes, I met the investor, and the investor was us—the collector and the dealer—not the outside opportunist.

THE BIG PICTURE

Fundamental to the stamp boom of the 1970s was the behavior of the underlying economy. Rampant inflation set in motion a broad tide that lifted all boats. The broad tide had more to do with why stamps rose so precipitously in price than did their innate attributes. To understand what caused the tide of inflation and the appetite for tangibles, we must look back in time.

Until the twentieth century, the world economy consisted of fiercely self-interested nation states operating according to the mercantilist principle, which was to accumulate as much gold as possible. Nations and businesses alike settled accounts in gold. The more gold a nation possessed, the more currency (gold coin) it could circulate, the more robust its economy and the more it prospered. Since gold served as currency, when a nation lost a significant amount of gold through trade deficits, its circulating currency shrank, reducing employment and prosperity. The mercantilist system functioned as a great incentive to be productive and to trade shrewdly. Nations with trade surpluses accumulated gold and enjoyed prosperity—Great Britain foremost among them.

The world economy began to evolve into its modern form during the heyday of the British Empire, between about 1815 and World War I. During that time Great Britain became the world's dominant industrial and military power. It built a global empire, accumulated great wealth, and in the process, a reputation for financial strength and stability. The pound sterling functioned as *the* medium of international exchange. Gold sovereigns, bearing the portrait of Queen Victoria, circulated throughout the empire and the world. And in the sunshine of this great prosperity, London grew to become the undisputed financial center of the world. It provided investment capital to finance growth abroad and acted as a clearing house for business and financial transactions from all parts of the globe. In effect, Britain became the world's banker.

Britain prospered until World War I, which proved too costly even for a nation as rich and powerful as she. By the time it was over, the war had drained her of her wealth, sapped her financial vitality, and ended her role as the world's dominant economic power. The United States—which had remained largely introverted during the nineteenth century, preoccupied with nation building, a civil war, and westward expansion—emerged as the strapping new economic power. But it possessed neither the international financial network nor the desire to fill the void created by Britain's weakness and decline. America—scarcely touched by the war—seemed content to go its own merry way, reveling in the boundless prosperity of the Roaring Twenties, which seemed as if it might go on forever.

Britain never regained her former glory and power. She limped through the 1920s, aided little by meager reparations from a destitute Germany, which had been stripped bare of capital and devastated by hyper-inflation. Things were not as rosy elsewhere in the world as they were in America and that, too, came to an end with the stock market crash of 1929.

After the stock market crash and the European financial crisis in 1931, nations turned inward and became increasingly protectionist, causing international trade to contract violently. Production plummeted, unemployment soared, bankruptcies skyrocketed and economic depression followed.

Economic thinkers were just beginning to appreciate the notion that national economies were inextricably linked together, that the health of individual national economies affected the health of the international economy as a whole. These thinkers—John Maynard Keynes foremost among them—viewed mercantilism, punitive reparations, and trade wars as destructive. Economic distress, Keynes warned, ultimately caused political instability and social upheaval, leaving desperate populations little choice other than to turn to communism, socialism, or fascism to restore economic and social stability. And the situation in Germany seemed to bear him out.

In America, the newly elected Franklin D. Roosevelt promoted an economic recovery program known as the New Deal to stimulate employment, which Keynes maintained was the key to prosperity and growth. Keynes opposed the gold standard (currencies backed by gold) because it caused nations with trade deficits to draw down their gold reserves to settle their debts, which contracted the amount of currency they could issue and circulate, which in turn shrank the money supply, increased unemployment and brought hard times. Keynes favored paper currency, unfettered by the constraints of gold, as the key to full employment and prosperity. He believed that government could cure economic distress by injecting money into the economy, thereby stimulating it. Just prime the pump, Keynes counseled, and the rest would take care of itself. Government should deficit spend (borrow money) to prime the pump—Keynes' theory held—then pay itself back during subsequent prosperity. In that way economic downturns could be moderated, if not eventually eliminated.

The New Deal went a long way toward helping America's ailing economy, but it was World War II that really stimulated employment, production, and created the prosperity that put America back on its feet. In the process, it turned America into the world's dominant industrial power.

Mindful of the disorder in the world economy that followed World War I—the destructive policy of reparations, inflation, high unemployment, depression, and social upheaval—economic thinkers all over the world began to understand the necessity for economic order after the conclusion of this second great war. Without some mechanism for stability, they feared another worldwide depression accompanied by political instability and possible military confrontation. So, in July 1944, delegates from 44 nations met in Bretton Woods, New Hampshire, to create a stable economic climate for the postwar world and facilitate international trade, which was vital to the health of all economies.

From the Bretton Woods meeting arose the International Monetary Fund (IMF) and International Bank for Reconstruction and Development (known as the World Bank). The IMF was created to formulate and enforce rules trading nations could live with, as well as provide access to automatic credits (a general line of credit, as it were) so that members would not have to depend on private-sector banks or on loans from other governments in times of financial distress. The World Bank was created to provide loans to rebuild the devastated nations of Europe and to provide loans to emerging nations for specific projects such as manufacturing plants or dams.

In order to borrow from the World Bank, a country had to be a member of the IMF, in which was vested the authority to police the trade practices and monetary practices of members—in other words, ensure their good behavior. Bretton Woods attendees anticipated that the availability of credit and the oversight of the IMF would do away with pre-war practices of currency devaluation, protectionism, and other potentially destructive actions nations took to gain advantages over trading competitors.

In addition to the IMF and World Bank, the United States, through the Marshall Plan, provided billions of dollars to the war-ravaged nations of Europe. Without access to credit, they would have been forced to pay for reconstruction and imports with dwindling gold reserves and in the process bankrupt themselves. And without foreign markets, the U.S. would have had to reduce production, which could easily have precipitated a recession, or even another depression. The international postwar recovery and the prosperity that followed would not have been possible without the IMF, the World Bank, and the Marshall Plan.

The two main players at Bretton Woods were the British representative, John Maynard Keynes, and the U.S. representative, Harry D. White, chief technical advisor to Secretary of the Treasury Henry Morgenthau. Keynes' main agenda was to create an international safeguard for full employment and to look after Britain's interests as a debtor nation. White's agenda was to look after America's interests as a creditor nation.

White wanted strict conditions attached to IMF money. He wanted to make sure that nations that drew IMF money could be required to take unpleasant and unpopular domestic measures, such as raising interest rates and cutting spending, to straighten out their financial affairs. IMF money was not to be welfare, but a means to allow a nation to catch its breath and solve its financial problems without creating a potentially destructive disruption in the international economy. White made it clear that the United States would call the shots on how the IMF was organized, and how it would be run. The United States would retain veto power over major IMF policy decisions—and no one was in a position to argue.

It was clear at Bretton Woods that America was the only major power capable of financing postwar reconstruction. It had replaced Great Britain as the financial center of the world, largely as a result of having financed the war with loans and aid. The United States also supplied most of the capital for the World Bank. America had become creditor to the world and in the process, the dollar had become the international currency. No other currency could match its historical integrity or its economic underpinnings, the backing of the most powerful military and industrial apparatus on earth.

Keynes lobbied hard for policies that favored his theories, most important of which was the "paper standard," currency not backed by gold, but only the good faith of the issuing nation. Needless to say, private bankers were mistrustful (and perhaps rightly so) of any government's ability to exercise fiscal self-restraint. The powerful New York banking community was skeptical of Keynesian notions in general and of the paper standard in particular. The so-called paper standard (which bankers regarded as no standard at all) seemed to be an open invitation to print as much currency as expedient for whatever purpose. Nor were bankers keen on the idea of any international entity that encroached on their banking turf.

Eventually, White and Keynes reached a compromise, a dollar redeemable in gold by governments, but not by individuals. A dollar redeemable in gold at the rate of $35 per ounce, the 1934 price. A dollar co-equal to gold for purposes of international commerce.

The Bretton Woods dollar/gold-exchange system allowed for the creation of money, while at the same time permitting settlement in the time-honored method—gold. In effect, the Bretton Woods Agreement formalized the dollar's role as the world's currency.

Central banks of most countries held dollars as part of their reserves, their faith in the United States so great that rarely did they redeem them for gold. A torrent of dollars flowed out of the United States in the form of aid and loans, payments for military bases, and investments by U.S. businesses and corporations. The flood of dollars stimulated the international economy, and kept stimulating it.

In no time at all, the United States found itself incurring a balance of payments deficit, i.e. it was spending more abroad than it was taking in. And the deficits continued year after year. You might say that the world's postwar prosperity was built on the U.S. balance of payments deficit.

Unfortunately, the dollar/gold exchange system contained one glaring defect—while the United States could create as many new dollars as it wanted, the amount of gold on reserve did not grow proportionately. By 1961, the amount of dollars abroad began to surpass the amount of gold in the U.S. Treasury and that triggered speculation in gold on overseas markets. President Kennedy tried to calm nervous financial markets by assuring them that the United States would stand behind the Bretton Woods agreement to redeem dollars in gold, but despite his assurances, gold redemptions increased and U.S. reserves shrank, which only made the problem worse.

Financial markets around the world saw the handwriting on the wall. Sooner or later, either the U.S. would have to curtail creating new dollars, which would cause an international economic contraction, or suspend redeeming dollars in gold, which would precipitate an international financial crisis.

By the mid-1960s the U.S. balance of payments deficits had skyrocketed. Although the deficit was partially attributable to the war in Vietnam, other more profound factors were at work. Germany and Japan, with dynamic reborn economies, increasingly cut into American markets both domestic and foreign. Americans began to see more and more foreign cars on the road, and notice more and more foreign consumer electronics on store shelves. And Lyndon Johnson's policy of financing both a war and a huge expansion in domestic social spending without raising taxes ignited inflation. The government ran huge deficits, but kept interest rates low and the economy humming by printing (borrowing) more and more money.

Foreign governments, which up until that time had been content to hold dollars, began to think it wiser to redeem them for gold. U.S. gold reserves plummeted. Although the U.S. continued to stand by its Bretton Woods pledge, everyone realized it could not do so indefinitely. The concept of a dollar co-equal to gold was dying.

The only reason America found itself able to continue to run huge balance of payment deficits was that its currency functioned as the international currency. It continued to create as many dollars as it needed for its domestic purposes. In doing so—by inflating the dollar—it began to export its domestic inflation overseas.

Charles De Gaulle, then president of France, decried the U.S. privilege of being able to fund its balance of payment deficits by printing more and more dollars. He demanded a return to an international gold standard, and when he didn't get it, he began redeeming France's dollar reserves for gold.

A panicky Treasury, pointing out that France's raid on America's gold reserves could trigger a stampede that would have disastrous economic implications for the entire world, quickly convinced its allies to create a gold pool to support redemptions of the dollar, and thus reassure nations that might otherwise have followed France's lead in making a run on the yellow metal. The Treasury, in effect, borrowed gold from other IMF members to meet redemptions. In theory, the gold was to be replaced later, during periods of low demand. At the same time, the Treasury began selling bonds denominated in foreign currencies to reduce overseas holdings of dollars. It encouraged the IMF to create SDRs (Special Drawing Rights), which were intended to replace the dollar as international currency, and thus remove the pressure the inflated dollar exerted on the international monetary system. But SDRs merely supplemented dollars and gold rather than replacing them, and didn't solve the problem. What bankers feared at the time of Bretton Woods had become reality—the world was being flooded by paper money.

The glut of dollars increased daily. The more dollars the U.S. pumped out, the less they were worth. The value of the dollar in comparison to other currencies was artificially high and, in normal circumstances would have been ripe for devaluation, but IMF protocols controlled the value of all major currencies in relation to one another, so the dollar remained at its artificially high level. The U.S. balance of payments deficit continued to rise. World financial markets fretted. The international currency was in the hands of a power, which rather than understand its special role and act responsibly, showed no interest in self-restraint and little interest in the negative effects of its actions. More and more, the United States, which had been held in such high esteem after the war, was perceived as having abused its special position. Resentment and concern grew in foreign capitals.

The root cause of the dollar's problem, declining international competitiveness, chronic balance of payments deficits, and deficit spending to finance both a war and expanded domestic social programs, only grew worse with the passing of time. These problems were not attributable to any particular presidential administration for they all had become thoroughly wedded to the philosophy that government should spend and could do so with impunity. No one seemed able to see beyond the immediate and the expedient—or care. No one seemed to sense the long-term danger of too many dollars.

Richard Nixon reacted to the recession of 1970—which he found politically painful—by becoming a born-again Keynsian. He prevailed upon his newly appointed Federal Reserve Chairman, Arthur Burns, to loosen money and stimulate the domestic economy.

During the Johnson years, Treasury Undersecretary Robert Roosa had carefully cobbled together a system of foreign central bank intervention and support for the dollar, which worked because it was mutually beneficial to both the U.S. (as creators of dollars) and its allies (as holders of dollars). Nixon and his Treasury Secretary, John Connelly, chose not to continue that close cooperation. They blamed the balance of payments deficit on the dollar being overvalued—a consequence of the fixed exchange rate mandated by the Bretton Woods agreement—rather than on the root causes. Clearly—Nixon felt—the answer was to devalue the dollar, but at the same time, he worried that it would be regarded as a sign of weakness, so he abandoned the idea.

By 1971, continuing balance of payments deficits and the Fed's easy money policy had caused further inflation and further erosion in the value of the dollar. Foreign speculators, sensing that the dollar would have to be revalued sooner or later, began dumping dollars. European central banks supported the dollar (bought dollars) as long as they could, but finally they had to throw in the towel. The selling frenzy proved too much for them. In August 1971, Nixon announced that the United States would henceforth no longer redeem dollars for gold, pulling the rug out from under the Bretton Woods agreement. In addition, he slapped a ten-percent surcharge on imports and imposed price controls. The dollar had become a 100 percent "paper standard" currency.

Closing the gold window sent shock waves through the world's financial community. The world's banker had just defaulted on backing its currency—the world's currency. And the import surcharge infuriated the Europeans and Japanese, but there was nothing they could do about it.

During the 1960s, the Europeans and Japanese had begun to have misgivings about the way the United States handled its financial affairs: its deficits, its lack of fiscal restraint, the way it managed its economy. They worried because the dollar functioned as the international currency, and because they held dollars. Historically, whenever the Europeans and Japanese got too nervous, Treasury officials had been quick to reassure them that everything was under control and that things would work out. So the Europeans and Japanese, like a banker holding a shaky loan, smiled, tried to ignore their misgivings, and hoped for the best.

Closing the gold window changed all that. Foreign financial markets realized they could no longer rely on the dollar or be sure how the United States would behave. The stage was set for the rampant inflation of the 1970s and the international free-for-all that followed.

In December 1971, Nixon revalued gold from $35 to $38 an ounce, thus devaluing the dollar by 8½ percent. Smart money, however, had stopped trusting "remedies" after the gold window closed the previous August. Nixon's devaluation triggered another wave of currency speculation against what the market perceived as the weak currencies—the dollar and the British pound. The pound went down in flames first. By mid-1972, after spending more than $2.5 billion supporting it, the British government threw up its hands and let the pound float.

Despite Nixon's remedies, the U.S. balance of payments deficit showed no sign of improving and inflation continued unabated. By early 1973, the most massive flight out of the dollar the world had ever seen got under way. German, Swiss and Japanese central banks bought dollars (more than $8 billion worth) in a desperate attempt to prop it up, but they could not begin to absorb the torrent of surplus dollars.

On February 12, 1973, the United States officially devalued the dollar by another 10 percent, but the action came too late. Foreigners no longer trusted Washington. The run against the dollar continued unabated. Central banks absorbed another $4 billion expatriate dollars to no avail. They simply did not possess the resources to absorb the endless sea of dollars being dumped by private banks, corporations, individuals, and even overseas branches of U.S. banks. On March 2, 1973, major central banks suspended all foreign exchange transactions. They remained closed for an astonishing two and a half weeks, while finance ministers and central bankers huddled to solve the crisis. When foreign exchange markets finally reopened, currencies were allowed to float. Central banks had come to the conclusion that currency supports were futile and decided to let nature take its course. During the following week, the dollar lost another 10 percent. The postwar era of the stable dollar was over.

No one wanted U.S. dollars or dollar-denominated financial instruments or securities. Knowledgeable buyers wanted German marks (strong economy and aversion to inflation) and Swiss francs (fiscal conservatism and partial backing of the franc by gold). Nervous investors around the world wanted their financial assets in currencies that functioned as reliable stores of value.

Then, as if things weren't bad enough, along came the oil shock of 1973. Skyrocketing oil prices drained even more dollars out of the United States, dramatically increasing the costs of domestic businesses, simultaneously causing both recession and inflation—an effect that would come to be known as stagflation. Worried that the United States would resort to paying for increasingly expensive oil by printing more dollars, Arabs opted for gold. Smart money the world over began to turn to gold. Central banks began increasing their gold reserves, which put tremendous pressure on the gold market. The price of gold climbed.

The oil-induced recession of 1974-75 lingered like a bad cold into the beginning of the Carter administration. Unemployment stood at seven percent. Carter desperately wanted to pull the nation out of recession. So, like his predecessors, he primed the pump by increasing government spending. Smart money across the world realized that meant more inflation and an even weaker dollar. So they bet against the dollar. They bought German marks, Swiss francs, Japanese yen and gold. Lots of gold.

In fairness, Carter did not create the situation he found himself in as much as inherit it. Still, when it came to solving the problem, he was out of his depth more than any president since World War II, and his ineptitude terrified foreign financial markets.

At the meeting of the Organization for Economic Cooperation and Development (OECD) in Europe in June 1977, Carter's Treasury Secretary W. Michael Blumenthal informed the Germans and Japanese that they should help pull the world out of recession by stimulating their economies with increased government spending. The Germans were aghast; they were not about to embark on any course of action even remotely inflationary. Not after their experience with hyperinflation in 1923. The Japanese economy was already booming because of exports of automobiles and consumer electronics to the U.S.; they saw no reason to artificially stimulate it. To make matters worse, Blumenthal told them that the United States would address the problem by reflating its economy unilaterally if necessary, an action that would further decrease the value of the dollar—and their dollar holdings.

Perhaps most shocking to OECD leaders was Blumenthal's attitude toward them. From the end of World War II, U.S. Treasury Secretaries had consistently reassured them about the value of the dollar whenever it had been in doubt. Not only did Blumenthal not reassure them, he in essence threatened to further devalue the dollar by reflating the U.S. economy. Where once there had been cooperation, now it seemed more like confrontation.

Blumenthal's performance at OECD removed any lingering trace of trust or goodwill and ignited yet another round of speculation against the dollar. The proximate cause was Blumenthal's performance at the OECD conference; the underlying cause was the mistrust of America's ability to manage its financial affairs. No sooner had he finished speaking at OECD than the electronically intertwined financial markets began to react. Flight out of the dollar began in earnest—like an old-fashioned bank run. Sellers couldn't dump dollars fast enough.

Like any commodity, currencies react to the laws of supply and demand. The supply of hard currencies is finite. There weren't nearly enough marks, yen and francs to go around, so prices soared—panicky buyers seemed to want them at any price. Conversely, the dollar sank like a stone. Blumenthal's response was that the U.S. would not intervene to support the dollar, and the dollar continued to slide.

In the eighteen months following Blumenthal's speech and Carter's malign neglect, the dollar lost 66 percent of its value against the Swiss franc, 55 percent against the Japanese yen, and 35 percent against the German mark. OPEC threatened to increase oil prices to offset losses incurred by having to accept dollars in payment for oil. And when, at last, Blumenthal tried to calm the stormy seas, no one listened. Trust in U.S. policy had been rewarded with an inflated international currency, the closing of the gold window, official devaluation, the abandonment of fixed exchange rates, and as the last straw, the refusal of the U.S. to even try to support the floating dollar. International money markets were in no mood to listen to anything the United States in general, or Carter and Blumenthal, in specific had to say.

Carter seemed stunned by how badly foreign financial decision-makers viewed the dollar, which, in reality was nothing more than a reaction to his management—or mismanagement—of both the economy and economic relations with other nations. Inflation continued to rage and the dollar continued to weaken. Eventually, it seemed to dawn on him that the downward spiraling dollar could trigger a worldwide financial collapse. He announced that the

United States would support the dollar, raise interest rates, tighten money and cool inflation, which he perceived—belatedly—as the root problem. Although Carter's pronouncements were intended to reassure global financial markets, smart money shrugged them off as a palliative. They knew that U.S. deficit spending would continue to increase, that the supply of dollars would continue to grow ever larger. So they bet for their own self-interest—against the dollar—and the dollar continued to slide.

Carter fired Blumenthal. Still the dollar continued to slide. Inflation hit double digits. The mark, franc and yen soared in value. As the climate of uncertainty intensified, investors (central banks, private banks, Arabs, multinational corporations and individuals) turned more and more to gold, pushing its price from $200 to $450 an ounce by the end of 1979. The election campaign of 1980 and the prospect of four more years of Carter only heightened the level of anxiety. Everyone had begun to think in terms of worst case scenarios.

Then along came the second oil shock, precipitated by the fall of the Shah of Iran. Fearful of an oil shortage caused by decreased Iranian production, speculators set off a wave of panic buying in the spot oil market. Prices, which had been $14 a barrel in 1978, surged to $30 in 1980 and $40 by 1981. The second oil shock sucked even more dollars out the United States, adding about $40 billion to the Euromarket. The Euromarket is a vast pool (actually more like a sea) of several trillion dollars worth of "stateless money," dollars circulating outside the United States, which are known as Eurodollars. Foreign bankers found themselves awash in dollars, and didn't know what to do with them. No one—it seemed—wanted dollars, except third world nations.

Iran took U.S. hostages, the Soviet Union invaded Afghanistan. Everything seemed to be out of whack. No one knew what would happen next—hyperinflation, Fortune-500-company bankruptcies, bank failures, international economic collapse, recession, depression, social upheaval, war. Possibilities abounded, none of them good.

In October 1979, to dampen inflation, the Federal Reserve increased the discount rate (the rate at which they lend money to banks) from 11 percent to 12 percent—an unheard of level.

Despite the increase, credit expansion continued unabated. An inflationary mindset gripped America. Borrow as much as you can, buy tangible assets, and repay loans with future cheaper (or worthless) dollars. Corporate borrowing increased because of the fear that the government might impose price controls. Farmers bought land. Stamp dealers hoarded inventory.

Gold rose from $500 to $875, amid new fears of a superpower confrontation over oil in the Middle East, precipitated by events in Iran and Afghanistan. Central banks continued to increase their gold reserves, all of which put enormous pressure on the price of gold. At the same time, the Hunts tried to corner the silver market, driving the price to nearly $50 an ounce, and nearly succeeded.

Interest rates approached 20 percent and began pushing the nation into a recession, while speculation continued unabated, fueling inflation. The Federal Reserve was stymied because high interest rates, which traditionally cooled inflation, seemed to have no effect. It seemed as if the disease had finally developed resistance to the drug. People everywhere prepared for the worst.

In November 1979, in response to the seizure of American hostages, Carter froze Iranian assets in U.S. banks and their overseas branches. While this move was applauded by Americans, it sent new shock waves through the international financial community; they suddenly realized that all foreign deposits in U.S. banks were subject to the whim of a President. Arabs were particularly disturbed. They had been huge buyers of U.S. Treasury securities (helping finance the deficit), but after Carter froze Iranian assets, they stopped buying treasuries and switched to gold. The wholesale flight of Arab money left the Treasury little choice other than finance the deficit through monetary expansion (creating more dollars), which meant more inflation, a weaker dollar, and so on, and so on.

Dollars poured into the Euromarket, but what to do with them? Third world countries, who had absorbed so many dollars after the first oil shock, were, by this time, reeling from high interest rates and on the verge of default. The oil shock dampened demand for their exports while increasing their costs. Their revenues plunged as did their ability to service their loans. Especially troubling was the size of their outstanding debt held by private banks. Bankers worried that default of a Mexico or Brazil could trigger a chain reaction of bank failures and a global financial meltdown. The situation was so bizarre that it confounded even the most seasoned money managers. No one knew what would happen, so they planned for the worst. They bought gold—and tangibles. And so did the little guy.

The average American, too, had become infected with uncertainty and started to worry about runaway inflation and its effect on his savings and investments. Stocks were down in the dumps. Yields on CDs (certificates of deposit) and bonds were high—but not in real terms; interest rate minus inflation. Tangibles appeared to offer the best chance of preserving—and increasing—capital. And that's why tangibles—and especially stamps—increased in price so much during the late 1970s.

And now, as they say, for the rest of the story. Carter finally made a smart move. He appointed Paul Volcker, a no-nonsense inflation fighter, chairman of the Federal Reserve. In March 1980, Volcker imposed credit controls and at long last inflation began to ease. Unfortunately, Volcker's credit controls devastated the building and automobile industries, increased unemployment and set off a wave of bankruptcies. Recession set in. But on the bright side, Volcker's actions—tight money, high interest rates and credit controls—reassured foreign financiers and restored a modicum of stability to the world financial markets. Unfortunately for Carter, they had painful domestic side effects and terrible political consequences. He lost the election to Ronald Reagan in November 1980. Reagan—like Eisenhower, Kennedy and Johnson before him—reassured nervous markets. Financial decision makers perceived him as an able leader, a man in control of events, and almost overnight speculators began to shift from gold (and other tangibles) to dollar assets, eager to lock in high interest rates. Reagan and Volcker got inflation under control, interest rates down, and the economy humming. Prosperity returned as never before, lasting throughout the 1980s and 1990s. Investors once again gravitated toward financial assets—mutual funds, stocks, bonds, annuities. The stock market boomed, IRAs and 401(k)s swelled, brimming with securities. And in the rush, investors forgot that tangibles ever existed.

The Cold War is over, Germany is reunified, the Soviet Union has disintegrated, Eastern Europe is independent, and Iraq has been subdued. The world has largely stopped worrying about the old set of problems. They have not given much thought to new ones that still lie hidden beyond the horizon—the resurgence of a militant Iran—and possibly Iraq; the consequences of instability in Eastern Europe and the Balkans; the growth of the Russian nation; the rise of economic juggernauts in the Far East—and their subsequent faltering; the growing European economic hegemony of a united Germany; the consequences of a fragile world burdened with too much population. Some economic thinkers wonder if the Euro (the European currency) will eventually replace the dollar as the *de facto* international currency, and if it does, what long-term effect that will have on the U.S. economy.

But answers to those questions lie in the future, their impact not discernable at this time.

THE STAMP MARKET

Great Britain issued the first postage stamp in 1840, a simple black affair featuring the profile of a young Queen Victoria and the denomination of one penny. It became known as the Penny Black. The United States followed suit in 1847 with its first general issue, a five-cent stamp featuring Benjamin Franklin and a ten-cent stamp featuring George Washington. And almost since the moment the first stamps appeared, people have been collecting them.

In addition to being one of the oldest hobbies, stamp collecting—or philately as it is known—is one of the largest and most well-established, boasting millions of collectors and thousands of dealers worldwide.

Stamp collectors are visually oriented. Aesthetics usually attracts them to stamps, and often after the initial encounter, they find themselves wanting to know everything about a stamp—what it is, where it comes from, when it was made, which details—if any—distinguish it from others of similar appearance. They're concerned with its condition, whether it's been altered, its rarity, and its value. They want to know about its place in history and perhaps most importantly, how it will fit in their collection. Collectors pay great attention to detail—the type of printing, type of paper, type of watermark, type of perforations, centering, and hinging, all of which have a bearing on value. They tend to be precise and analytical in describing these details and as a result, philately has developed an extensive technical vocabulary. Philately has also produced a massive body of literature—tens of thousands of books—covering just about every aspect of stamp collecting in copious detail.

The hobby supports two weekly newspapers, more than half a dozen major monthly publications, dozens of regularly published club and society journals, and several catalogue publishing companies. Dealers operate in most major cities and many smaller towns across the country. And not a week goes by without several public auctions or stamp shows.

The majority of stamp collectors tend to be well educated and affluent. They buy primarily for enjoyment. They generally start by accumulating low-cost material, sorting it, organizing it, and learning about the hobby. As their interest matures, their mode of collecting often dovetails with other inclinations. Some enjoy the thrill of the hunt, some enjoy the competition of exhibiting, some enjoy research and discovery, while others find the social interaction with fellow collectors to be the most enjoyable aspect of the hobby. Whatever the reason, stamp collectors collect because it's fun.

Collectors become attached to their stamps. They're rarely inclined to part with them. Stamps in collections typically disappear from the market for years, in many cases not reappearing until the collector dies. Collectors purchase stamps in good times and in bad. Historically, the stamp market has been stable because collectors purchase stamps irrespective of the economic conditions and because they rarely sell in response to market fluctuations.

How large is the stamp market? At one point, the Postal Service estimated that 22 million Americans collected stamps, a figure now generally regarded as exaggerated. A more recent and careful analysis estimates that about 150,000 serious collectors form the core of philately in the United States. These collectors add to their collections regularly, belong to a stamp club or national philatelic society, or subscribe to one or more philatelic periodicals. The analysis suggests that a second tier of less committed collectors exists, also numbering about 150,000. This group remains largely invisible. They obtain many of their stamps directly from the post office or from mail order dealers. They don't belong to philatelic societies or organizations, attend stamp shows, or subscribe to philatelic publications.

Another 5 million to 6 million collectors are estimated to exist beyond the second tier, but they operate at the very fringes of philately. They buy infrequently and only stamps that strike their fancy, such as Elvis stamps or Princess Diana stamps. They typically buy directly from the post office or from novelty advertisements such as those appearing in Sunday newspaper supplements. They tuck their purchases in boxes and drawers rather than mount them in albums. They don't patronize stamp dealers for older stamps, attend stamp shows or subscribe to philatelic publications. They're not much of a factor in the secondary market.

The stamp market is old and well established, but it differs—as do other collectibles markets—from financial markets and therefore, does not behave in the same way.

The most significant way in which the stamp market differs from financial markets is that collectors buy for enjoyment rather than profit.

The stamp market and financial markets differ in other respects as well. Securities are fungible, stamps are not. Any share of a stock is identical to all other shares of the same class. They do not need to be authenticated, graded or even held in physical form, and they can be traded sight unseen.

Stamps differ from one another. Each is graded according to its individual merits—centering, gum, color, perforations, faults, etc. Each is priced according to its merits and the range of prices varies dramatically—from as little as five or ten percent of catalogue for a defective copy, to as much as double or triple catalogue for a superlative copy, and innumerable price shadings exist for condition grades in between. Because price is a function of condition, buyers insist on seeing stamps. As a result, stamps are generally not traded sight unseen.

Financial securities trade on well-established, easily accessible, highly centralized markets. An order placed anywhere in the world can be transmitted electronically, and buyer and seller know immediately how much they have paid or will be paid. Data on the market is available instantaneously and summaries of prices and volume are published daily in newspapers.

The stamp market is not highly centralized. Thousands of individual dealers across the country and around the world buy and sell stamps based on their own experience, financial ability, and customers' needs. Dealers buy according to their own opinion of grade, which is subjective, and necessarily so. Both retail and buying prices vary from dealer to dealer, although virtually all use one or more of the standard catalogues as a basic reference point. Catalogues—analogous to securities price listings that appear in the financial sections of newspapers—usually publish updated prices only once a year. The market relies on more informal means—dealer price lists, retail ads and buying ads in stamp periodicals—for up-to-date information about prices.

Financial markets trade huge volumes and institutional investors play a major role. The stamp market is small by comparison and the size of typical transactions, minuscule by comparison. Institutional investors play no role in the stamp market.

Financial markets are more volatile and frenetic than collectibles markets. Like hyperactive children, they just can't seem to sit still. They respond to every scrap of information and rumor almost as if the fate of the world depended on it. A quarter-point change in interest rates or a hiccup in employment statistics can trigger a stampede of buying or a mad dash for the exits.

Things happen much more slowly in the stamp market. Stamp dealers are not particularly concerned about day-to-day—let alone minute-by-minute—price changes. The stamp market plays the tortoise, to the stock market's hare.

Financial markets have developed sophisticated analytical tools, even developed computer generated programs for buying and selling. They scrutinize these numerical bones to divine the future much as the shaman scrutinizes the animal bones.

The stamp market lacks truly sophisticated analytical tools and functions just fine without them. Several attempts have been made to establish a centralized stamp exchange, but none succeeded. The mentality of those who participate in the stamp market is not the same as those who participate in financial markets.

The two markets are dissimilar, yet each has evolved in response to the specific needs of its participants and each serves its constituency well.

Why compare the two markets? Because there is a tendency to become fuzzy headed when considering stamps as investments and to begin thinking about them as if they were financial assets, which they are not. The stamp market should not be approached as if it were a financial market. It should be approached on its own terms and accepted for what it is.

Markup

Stamps differ from financial investments in another important respect—one that is usually glossed over or ignored by stamp investment books—and that is the size of the markup. Markup is the difference between what a dealer pays for a stamp and what he sells it for.

Most financial investments trade with only a negligible transaction cost, usually expressed as a commission, load, or bid/ask spread. The transaction cost of buying $5,000 worth of common stock (e.g., 100 shares at $50 each) is as little as $25-$50 depending upon whether you use an electronic broker or a traditional broker. It amounts to one percent or less. Assuming the same cost when selling, the stock need only rise in price a dollar a share to break even and start showing a profit.

Markups on precious-metal bullion coins and bars typically range from three to five percent and are usually expressed as buy/sell spreads. A buy/sell spread of $405/$425 on a one-ounce gold coin amounts to just under five percent. The same small transaction costs apply to most other types of investments found on the financial pages.

Collectibles rarely trade on the basis of commissions or buy/sell spreads. They're purchased at one price and sold at another. The difference between the two prices is markup. Markups are usually significantly higher than transaction costs for financial assets.

One of the most difficult things for those outside the trade to understand is that there is no standard markup in the stamp business. It varies from dealer to dealer, from item to item, and from time to time.

Having said that, and having spent a lifetime in the stamp trade, let me say that markups tend to be about 100 percent for mid-range items—items retailing in the $20 to $500 range. A stamp purchased for $20 will likely retail for $40. Markups range from as little as five or ten percent at the top end of the market to as much as 300 percent to 1,000 percent at the low end—the nickel-and-dime stamps, and this in order to make them even marginally profitable.

A few years back a would-be dealer decided to get into the business of selling used stamps of the world. He obtained his stock by soaking bulk mixtures and carefully mounting each stamp on a retail card. He pointed out with great pride that a $20 mixture yielded more than $200 in retail value.

"The markup is fantastic!" he said. After several months preparing his inventory, he took a table at one of the local stamp shows.

"How'd you do?" I asked after the show was over.

"Not bad," he said. "Made about two hundred bucks."

"In sales or profit?"

"Sales."

His table had cost $100. His "profit" of $100 could not even begin to have adequately compensated him for the hours he'd spent preparing the stamps for sale, to say nothing of the sixteen hours he'd put in at the booth. He showed up at a couple more shows, grossing about $200 at each. He was unemployed at the time, and had hopes of making stamps a career, but his approach was a losing proposition. After a few shows, he faded from the scene. He learned the hard way that large markups by themselves do not necessarily lead to big profits.

Markup is not the same as profit. The costs of delivering a stamp to the consumer (overhead, advertising, operating supplies, insurance, wages, travel, bourse fees, accounting fees, taxes, interest, and so forth) must be subtracted from markup to arrive at net profit. There is a tendency in the collecting community to condemn the dealer for doubling his money, for making $20 on a $40 sale. The perception is that the dealer is ripping off the collector. But that's simply not the case. In reality, net profits usually amount to about ten to fifteen percent after subtracting expenses—that's $10-$15 on a $100 sale. As a dealer friend of mine is fond of saying, "Stamp dealers aren't the ones building skyscrapers and driving Mercedes."

Markups on high-priced stamps, such as Zeppelins, are usually less—often ten to twenty percent—than on inexpensive stamps. It's not uncommon for a dealer to pay something like $1,500 or $1,600 for a set of Zeppelins that he's retailing for $2,000.

Stamp dealers are notoriously tight lipped about markup, in part due to the public perception that the difference between cost and retail is all profit and in part because they do business among themselves and don't want to reveal anything that might give a competitor a negotiating advantage.

Dealers buy from a variety of sources—auctions, collectors, and fellow dealers—and in the process pay a variety of prices. They buy based on their clientele, their knowledge of stamps, their access to material, and their capitalization. Their situations vary, as do their outlooks and styles of doing business, all of which influence their approach to pricing. The result is a mish-mosh of costs and markups that defy generalizing.

During the Great Boom, markups tightened considerably as the pace of buying and selling accelerated. Dealers worked on smaller margins—often ten to twenty percent—because they found they could earn greater profits by turning inventory rapidly than by holding out for the maximum markup. In this situation—low markups combined with rapidly rising stamp prices—investors found it easier to make profits on quick moves in and out than they could in a flat market.

The point is that the magnitude of markups for stamps (and other collectibles) profoundly differs from the transaction costs of financial investments. In the earlier example, we noted that a $5,000 block of stock need only rise $50-$100 in order to overcome the transaction cost. A $5,000 portfolio of stamps (100 stamps at $50 each) needs to rise to $10,000 to overcome a markup of 100 percent. In a stagnant market, that could take ten or twenty years. A rise in portfolio value from $5,000 to $7,500 looks pretty good on paper, but doesn't mean a profit. Fifty percent of $7,500 is only $3,750 or $1,250 short of the original price.

There's a tendency to regard increases in catalogue price or market price as profit, when often it is not. Profit is liquidation price minus original cost.

As a rule of thumb, assume that most mid-range stamps are traded on the basis of a 100 percent markup. When buying retail, assume that you'll get about half if forced to sell right away.

By this time you're probably thinking, "Wow, buying stamps for investment doesn't make much sense." And it doesn't—*if you pay full retail.* The key to profit in any investment is the difference between the cost and the liquidation price. So the idea is to buy right, to buy for less than retail, to buy as close to "wholesale" as possible. And that means doing a little homework and keeping your eyes open for opportunities.

As part of your general strategy, learn what dealers pay for stamps. Get an idea by checking buy prices in wanted-to-buy ads in philatelic weeklies. Scanning wanted-to-buy ads also gives you a feel for what's in demand. Check buy prices against retail prices to get a better feel for markups (be sure you're comparing equivalent grades).

Read auction catalogues (the more the better), study prices realized, compare them to published buy prices. You'll begin to discover where buying opportunities exist. For example, if you buy a stamp at auction for $55 that normally sells for $100 retail, you've just trimmed 90 percent off the markup. Now your investment need only rise $5 instead of $50 in order to start making money.

"Why would a stamp sell so cheaply?" you ask. The answer is that a few lots slip through the cracks at every auction. There are bargains to be had. That's why so many dealers bid at auction. More about that in the chapter on buying. The point is to be aware of markup and its impact on profits.

Speaking of slipping through the cracks, the value of knowledge in stamp investing can never be stressed enough. Consider the collector who found a used copy of the rarest variety of the one-cent issue of 1851 in a dealer's counter box at Pacific 97. The stamp was priced at $15—it catalogued $29,000 at the time! He spotted it because of his knowledge and no doubt because it was so rare that all who had previously looked at it—including the dealer—assumed it was the common variety. He profited from his investment in knowledge.

Another fellow spotted a rare color-omitted production error in a pile of mint sheets on a dealer's table at a show. He bought the sheet for $5 (its face value) and sold it later that same day for $20,000! The error was so subtle that everyone else had missed it, except the knowledgeable buyer. When it comes to stamps, knowledge is most definitely power.

Sometimes one hears the complaint that books cost money. Books have never cost me a penny—they've made me money. The payoff comes in the opportunities that knowledge provides. In addition, philatelic books are often good investments in themselves. Most philatelic books are produced in small numbers and once out of print are often worth more than their original cost. When philatelic libraries appear at auction, they invariably attract great interest and strong bidding. Never underestimate the value of knowledge.

In summary, the investor must address the cost of markup in his strategy. He must understand that it varies, that it can be substantial, and he must strive to reduce its impact on his purchases. Buy right. This cannot be emphasized enough, for above all, buying right is the key to profit in stamp investing.

BASIC ECONOMICS

Over the years, I've been struck by how often stamp investors lack even a bare-bones grasp of economics, the fundamentals that affect the behavior and value of their investments. We'll review the fundamentals in this chapter to once again bring into focus the factors that make prices rise and fall.

Economics has been defined as the study of the allocation of resources to satisfy human wants. This is accomplished through trading—exchanging goods and services. Human beings are by nature trading creatures. Most other creatures each satisfy their own individual needs such as food, water, and shelter. They do not exchange goods and services, although a few cooperate to one degree or another (e.g., wolves in packs, bees in hives). We humans, on the other hand, are trading fools; we live to trade. We spend our days earning money—by creating or helping to create goods and services—that we exchange for other goods and services—food, clothing, books, travel, entertainment, education, automobiles, and so forth. And when we're not actually trading, we're often thinking about trading—that new car we've had our eye on, a Caribbean vacation, landscaping the yard or a thousand other things.

To satisfy our proclivity to trade we have developed a highly complex and specialized system—the economy—and a number of sophisticated tools to facilitate commerce—money, credit, markets, and foremost among them, money. Here are the basics.

Value. Economics teaches us that goods possess one or more possible types of value. The most fundamental value is utilitarian value (use value). Food, water, clothing and shelter have utilitarian value. They satisfy our most basic survival needs. Other types of value (and there are more than those mentioned here) include market value, exchange value, book value, perceived value, and in the case of stamps, catalogue value.

The utilitarian value of a mint, never-hinged 50-cent Zeppelin stamp of 1933 is fifty cents—its face value.

At this writing, its catalogue value is $120.

Its retail value—according to a retail advertisement in one of the stamp weeklies—is $100.

Its wholesale value—according to a buy ad in the same paper—is $60.

To the collector whose grandmother obtained it at the Chicago World's Fair in 1933 and passed it down to him, it has immeasurable sentimental value.

Already, the stamp has five possible values—and perhaps others as well. Investors value stocks in a variety of ways—book value, future earnings value, PE (price/earnings) ratio value, and so forth. Investors purchase stocks—or any other investment—because they perceive present market value to be less than one of the other values, be it book value, future earnings value, PE ratio value, speculative value, or whatever. Prices of stocks rise and fall in response to the demand based on investors' perceptions of value, rather than on any strictly quantifiable basis. The prices of stamps rise and fall in response to buyers' perceptions also. And perceptions vary over time.

Aside from utilitarian value, value tends to be fluid, intangible, and abstract rather than a fixed property. It arises from demand-based perception, which like beauty, lies in the eye of the beholder.

The point is to begin thinking about value in the abstract. Do not regard it as a fixed quantifiable property. It isn't. Regard it as a fluid property. That doesn't mean it's imaginary, it's not. But neither is it fixed. Just remember that value rests on the pedestal of demand, and that the pedestal of demand rests on the sands of perception. Value is a function of the willingness of buyers to buy.

Numerous unique stamps exist. Their prices range from less than a hundred dollars to nearly a million dollars.

When it comes to investment, the only value that counts is the market value on the day an asset is bought and the value on the day it is sold. All other values are hypothetical.

Price. Price is the figure at which a commodity trades. Like water, it always seek its own level, despite controls, treaties, or any other constraint.

Market. A market is a place where buyers and sellers meet to exchange commodities. Buyers and sellers meet face to face in some markets—flea markets, farmers markets, supermarkets, shopping malls—and indirectly in others—stock markets and commodity markets. Regardless of whether it has a physical locus or not, a market is a "place" where buyers get together to exchange money and goods.

The term "market" is also used in the sense of temperature of economic activity. When we ask, "How is the stamp market?" we want to know if stamp prices are rising, falling or steady; if the mood is optimistic or pessimistic; and if the pace of buying and selling is brisk or slow.

There is a tendency to think of markets as inanimate objects. Markets are, in fact, animate organisms composed of masses of *individual* human buyers—human beings who think and act like other human beings. Never forget that a market is nothing more than the aggregation of individual human minds operating in a fashion similar to yours. The perceptions, attitudes, and opinions of those individuals dictates the "market." When the aggregate is inclined to buy, prices rise. When it is inclined to sell, prices fall.

Individuals view events in relation to their impact on them and trends are as fragile as the perceptions of the players. Markets are inherently unpredictable because they are made up of individuals who tend to act in a predictable fashion, but not with predictable timing.

Demand. Demand is the desire to acquire a commodity for whatever reason. In the case of stamps, it can be based on utilitarian value (to mail a letter), collector value (for enjoyment), and/or speculative value (the prospect of making a profit). In the case of stamp dealers, demand arises from a desire to maintain a stock in trade.

Normally, collectors acquire stamps for enjoyment. In a speculative market, the emphasis shifts to financial gain.

In a non-speculative market, the equilibrium of supply and demand can be charted (price on the vertical axis, time on the horizonal axis) as a relatively flat horizontal line. The line rises gradually over time to take into account inflation, but for the most part remains relatively flat. In a speculative market, the graphed line moves up more sharply. The degree to which speculation affects the market is revealed by the steepness of the price curve as it rises above the extension of the normal equilibrium line.

Without demand, market value is hypothetical. When there's no demand for an item, supply (rarity) becomes irrelevant. Demand determines value, and it drives price.

Money. Money is most often defined as a medium of exchange and a store of value. When we buy things, we're doing nothing more than exchanging our goods and services (as represented by money) for the goods and services of others. Money merely facilitates the exchange, serves as an accounting tool.

The more convenient money is, the better it serves as a medium of exchange. Over the centuries and until recently, precious metals served as money because they were scarce and desirable in their own right. Later governments issued paper currency that represented reserves of precious metals. Today, most paper currencies are fiat currencies. They have no backing whatsoever and are money by virtue of government edict or "fiat." Our own currency says "This note is legal tender for all debts public and private." It is money because the government says it is, and because everyone accepts it as such.

Money also serves as a store of value, but it can depreciate and lose its purchasing power. This is the weakness of fiat money as a store of value.

The value of money, like any other commodity, is subject to fluctuation. Its value is affected by monetary and fiscal policy,

balance of trade surpluses or deficits, and of course, perception. In
the case of the Swiss franc in the late 1970s, demand for it as a
hard currency pushed its value abnormally high. Switzerland is a
small country of a few million people. It circulates a relatively
small amount of francs in comparison to the amount of dollars
circulated by the United States. When investors dumped dollars for
Swiss francs, the law of supply and demand pushed the price of the
franc far beyond what it might otherwise have been.

Purchasing Power. Purchasing power is the power of money
to buy commodities. The purchasing power of a dollar is three 32-
cent stamps, with four cents left over. Essentially, a dollar will
mail three first-class letters. Forty years ago, a dollar would mail
33 first-class letters. The purchasing power of a dollar has declined
from 33 letters to three letters. The utilitarian value of a three-cent
stamp has depreciated more than 90 percent.

Inflation. Several types of inflation exist but there is no need
to go into the technical differences here. The effect is the same,
the erosion of purchasing power. The relationship between goods
and money (which is expressed as price) constantly changes as
inflation rises.

Goods, on the other hand, tend to remain more stable in
relationship to one another. For example, forty years ago $3,000
bought a pretty nice car and $20,000, a pretty nice house. At this
writing a car and a house of similar quality cost about $30,000 and
$200,000 respectively. Each costs ten times as much as it did forty
years ago, yet their value relative to one another has remained
fairly constant. The car and the house increased ten times in
"value" only in terms of price. Since it takes ten times as much
money to buy either, a more realistic view is that the money has
depreciated by a factor of ten. The cruel paradox of inflation is
that people think they're earning more and that the value of their
assets is rising, while, in fact, the value of their money is going
down.

Inflation is endemic and chronic in all modern free economies.
Prevailing economic wisdom dictates that some inflation is
stimulative and therefore, beneficial—in the range of two or three

percent. Anything above that begins to trigger a spiral of wage and price increases as workers and businesses become inflation conscious. Then things begin to get out of control, as they did in the 1970s.

Workers and businesses tend to stay pretty much even with inflation through wage and price increases. Assets, too, tend to hold their value over time because they are useful or desirable in their own right. But savings held in the form of money are vulnerable to erosion. Interest offsets inflation only to the extent that the interest rate exceeds the rate of inflation. Ten percent interest minus nine percent inflation is not much of a return.

Inflation is dangerous because it erodes the purchasing power of fixed investments such as savings, bonds and pensions, cheating those, especially the elderly, who rely on them for income. After the Soviet Union collapsed in 1992, many pensioners found their life savings completely wiped out by inflation. Past their active earning years, they are now destitute.

The value of modern money relies completely on the ability of the issuing government to manage its financial affairs in a responsible manner. Those who have accumulated assets understand the ephemeral nature of government's attitude toward other people's money.

Tangible assets—such as stamps—are a hedge against inflation because they tend to hold their value in relation to other assets irrespective of changes in the purchasing power of money.

Investment and Consumption. One more thing while we're on the subject of basic economics. Understand that all purchases fall into one of two categories: investment or consumption.

Investments are purchases that have the potential to increase in value, such as real estate, stocks, bonds, and some stamps.

A purchase that increases the opportunity to make money, such as the subscription to a stamp periodical—although technically a consumption item because it can only be resold for less than its original cost—can be thought of as an "investment" because it can be used to increase one's ability to make money.

Consumption purchases are purchases that are used up over the course of their life, such as appliances, vacations, automobiles, and so forth. Sometimes sales pitches for consumer goods tout them as investments, when technically they are not. The test of an investment is, does it possess the potential to rise in value? Consumer goods generally do not possess that quality. Money spent on investment tends to multiply itself. Money spent on consumption simply evaporates. Foregoing consumption in favor of investment generally increases net worth.

Okay, those are the basics, now let's move forward.

CONDITION & GRADE

During the Great Boom, the term "investment grade" appeared on the scene almost overnight, and although never formally defined, was generally understood to mean any stamp in superior condition with potential for appreciation. By the end of the boom it had become little more than a cliche applied to almost any mint, never-hinged U.S. stamp issued before 1930.

What is an investment grade? The most important element of any stamp considered for investment is its potential for appreciation. Within the population of an item deemed to have potential for appreciation, the second vital element is condition.

Realtors have a saying that the three most important elements of value are "location, location, location." In stamps, the three most important elements of value are "condition, condition, condition."

Grading is the way in which condition is described, focusing primarily on centering and to a lesser degree, general appearance. Stamps are priced according to grade and prices vary dramatically. For example, ninety percent of the $5,500 price for a superb, mint $5 Columbian represents a premium for condition. The exact same stamp can be had for a few hundred dollars in seriously faulty condition. Anything you pay above the lowest grade is a premium for condition. When buying a stamp, you are buying condition.

The market is obsessed with quality. Buyers want the best—the best gum, the best margins, the best centering, the best color, the best of all condition elements. They abhor faults. The astute investor is wise to bear in mind the preferences of the market for material in his portfolio.

Margins. At minimum, a stamp should possess margins of at least normal size for its issue. Margins vary in size from issue to issue; early issues usually having the smallest ones. There is almost no space between some stamps, such as the three-cent issues of 1851 and 1857. Others, such as the U.S. parcel post issues of 1913, are spaced well apart and routinely encountered with visually appealing margins. Generally, a stamp possessing margins larger than normal for its issue—assuming they are balanced—is worth a premium. Dramatically oversized margins—referred to as "jumbo" or "boardwalk" margins—are especially prized.

Centering. Centering is the way in which a stamp's design is situated in relation to its margins. The more balanced the margins, the more visually appealing and desirable the stamp. Early stamps are notoriously poorly centered. Take this into account when assessing centering. Some nineteenth century stamps have almost no room between stamps, which results in perforations touching the design or cutting into it on at least one side. Experienced buyers understand that it is not always possible to find perfectly centered copies of some stamps and must content themselves with reasonably centered copies of such issues.

Familiarize yourself with the characteristic margins and centering of various issues in order to be able to recognize better than normal examples. Also bear in mind that modern stamps are usually well centered. Don't try to hold early issues to the same standard. Each issue must be assessed according to its own characteristics. Experienced buyers often turn stamps upside down or sideways to view centering from every possible angle.

Standard centering grades include extremely fine (XF, very well centered); very fine (VF, moderately centered); fine (F, poorly centered, perforations need only be clear of the design); and average (Avg, very poorly centered, perfs often cut into the design). These grades are illustrated in Figure 1. A variety of split grades, such as F-VF (fine to very fine), describe finer shadings. Superb (S) is used to describe gem copies in the highest state of perfection.

Figure 2. Standard centering grades from left to right include: average; fine; fine to very fine; very fine; and extremely fine.

Catalogues generally list prices for only one grade of centering, usually in the middle of the spectrum. Therefore, depending on the exact grade, the actual price of a given stamp may be higher or lower than catalogue price. Only a small fraction—perhaps as few as ten percent—of most earlier stamps exist in the grade listed and priced by catalogues.

Philatelic terms often have meanings specific to the hobby, while their counterparts in common usage have altogether different meanings. For example, the term "fine," as applied to stamp centering, has come to mean a poorly centered stamp. To be precise, its perforations need only clear the design. In reality, "fine" stamps are very unattractive. Yet in common usage "fine" refers to something of higher than normal quality. In fact, *Webster's New World Dictionary* defines "fine" as something that is "excellent" or "of superior quality." So, take time to familiarize yourself with the nuances of stamp grading terminology.

Gum and Hinging. Comments on gum apply to unused stamps. Used stamps are assumed to be without gum and it has no bearing on their value. The terms "mint" and "unused" are frequently used interchangeably, but in many cases "mint" is used to refer to a stamp that has never been hinged, and in some cases "unused" implies uncancelled but without gum. These nuances in usage are by no means universal so pay attention to the context in which a term is used. Check the "terms" section in the front of auction catalogues before bidding to see how they use the terminology.

Contemporary collectors prefer gum to be in the best possible condition and that means never-hinged (NH) stamps. Until the middle of the twentieth century, stamps were customarily mounted with hinges, which is why so few early stamps survive without hinge marks. Early hinges were often just regular bits of paper folded in half and attached—one side to the back of the stamp and the other to the album page—with whatever glue was handy. They were difficult to remove, often causing thins or disturbed gum when pulled off. Later, glassine hinges coated with light adhesives were developed and marketed to the hobby. Glassine hinges are much less likely to cause damage when removed; nevertheless, they do leave hinge marks.

Gum on unused stamps is graded according to its presence and on the severity of hinging. As with centering, the earlier the stamp, the less perfect the state of its gum.

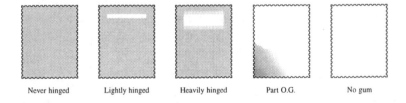

Never hinged   Lightly hinged   Heavily hinged   Part O.G.   No gum

Figure 2. Gum and hinging.

States of gum are described as follows. Standard abbreviations appear in parentheses.

Original gum (OG). Gum originally applied to the stamp.

Never-hinged (NH). Gum to which a stamp hinge has never been applied. Implies that gum is in the same state as when it left the post office. The most desirable condition.

Lightly hinged (LH). Gum bearing only the slightest evidence of having been hinged.

Heavily hinged (HH). Gum that has been disturbed by the removal of a hinge or that contains all or part of a hinge (referred to as a hinge remnant) so securely affixed that it cannot be removed without disturbing the gum. Dealers are often reluctant to remove hinges for fear of causing damage or ending up with gum that looks worse than if left alone.

Part (or partial) original gum. Only partial original gum remaining, usually on the lower half of the stamp, the top part most often missing as a result of hinge removal. A condition usually associated with and considered normal for pre-1890 unused stamps.

Disturbed gum (DG). Generally understood to mean gum disturbed by removal of a stamp hinge, but also applies to any form of gum damage, such as that arising from a stamp having been stuck down or stuck to another stamp. The term "glazed gum" refers to the glossy appearance resulting from gum having been somewhat liquified then stuck to a nonporous surface such as a plastic mount. The term "tropical gum" refers to gum that has been affected by humidity in a tropical or subtropical climate and thus lost its original texture.

No gum (NG). Without gum, usually understood to mean that gum has been removed unless qualified by "without gum as issued." Stamps lacking original gum usually sell for a small fraction of those possessing original gum. The absence of gum on stamps issued without gum does not detract from their value.

Regummed (RG). A stamp to which gum has been applied to simulate original gum. Regummed stamps are generally regarded as impaired goods and usually sell for a small fraction of those possessing original gum. It is not unlawful to regum stamps, but it is unethical to represent them as having original gum.

Gum skips. Natural gum skips are small areas on the back of a stamp not covered by gum at the time it was laid down during manufacture. Technically not a fault, gum skips generally don't affect a stamp's price unless they are large or unsightly.

As a rule, the earlier the stamp, the more severe the hinging. The gum on most nineteenth century stamps is either partially or completely missing, heavily hinged, or disturbed from hinge removal.

In the early days, gum was made up in batches and applied by hand with brushes, giving uneven results from one job to the next. After aging more than a century and a half, such gum has often cracked, browned, or otherwise degraded, and looks nothing like the pristine gum on modern stamps, the gum collectors are so accustomed to seeing and associating with premium quality stamps. When first encountering early original gum, the inexperienced eye often finds it so unappealing, so different from that found on modern issues that the initial impulse is to refuse to believe it is really original gum. One school of thought is that original gum used during the first 25 years of stamp manufacture is so ugly that its presence is unimportant anyway. Auctions frequently publish the disclaimer "original gum is not to be expected on stamps before 1890," and it is well to bear that in mind. Nineteenth century stamps possessing original gum are scarce, and those that do have it usually have been heavily hinged. Except for a few low denominations, never-hinged copies are, indeed, rare. Because only a minuscule percentage of key nineteenth century stamps—such as the high-value Columbians—are never-hinged, certification by a competent expertizing authority is essential for examples purporting to be never-hinged.

As with centering, the condition of gum on a stamp must be measured against others of its issue, not against modern issues. One must be forgiving about the condition of gum on early issues. The presence of any reasonably attractive gum—be it hinged or not—on pre-1870 stamps is a bonus. Light hinging is the best one can reasonably expect for most nineteenth century issues. Twentieth century stamps are generally available never-hinged, although light hinging is sometimes the best one can expect on the rarer issues.

Strive to obtain the best possible examples available. As a general rule, the higher the grade, the greater the premium for never-hinged condition. Do not pay a never-hinged premium for visually unappealing stamps and stamps in lower grades. They're not investment grade and generally of interest only to price conscious collectors looking to fill spaces at minimal cost.

Perforations. Collectors prefer reasonably intact and balanced perforation tips within the limits of an issue. Some U.S. issues, such as the hard-paper banknotes, are prone to irregular perfs because they were printed on brittle paper with poor separation characteristics. The 1875 reprints of the 1857-60 issue usually exhibit ragged, irregular, or short perfs because of the paper.

Others, such as perf 8½ or perf 10 Washington-Franklins, separate poorly due to the size or spacing of their perforation holes. Sometimes perforating equipment did not completely punch out holes, leaving them filled with circular bits of paper, which are unsightly. Assess the condition of perforations in context with that which is usual for an issue. Where irregular perfs are the norm—as they are on a majority of nineteenth century issues—they should not be considered a fault.

Short or pulled perfs—as opposed to irregular perfs—refers to perforation teeth that are missing, usually all the way to the base of the perforation or below it. Short perfs are generally considered a minor fault, unless they are characteristic of an issue.

Color. How vivid or pronounced color is within the range of shades typically encountered on an issue. Usually, the more intense the color, the more appealing the stamp. Collectors prefer color as near the issued state as possible, color that is fresh, bright, vivid, and intense. Some stamps—most notably orange-colored issues—tend to discolor when they come in contact with sulphur compounds, either atmospheric or in album or stockbook papers. Others, such as the 30-cent denomination of the 1861 series, are notoriously poorly colored. Again, a stamp's color must be measured against others of its kind, not against other issues that are routinely boldly colored.

Freshness. Ideally, a stamp possesses "mint bloom" and paper as fresh as the day it was printed. The older the stamp, the less likely one is to find it in a state of pristine freshness. Until the second half of the twentieth century, album manufacturers paid little attention to the quality of paper they used in making albums. As a result, stamps are often encountered with a slight brownish or yellowish cast (referred to as toning) from years or decades in albums or stockbooks made of low-grade paper. Toned stamps are visually unappealing and avoided by knowledgeable buyers. Again, the degree of freshness must be measured against that which is usual for an issue.

Cancels. The ideal cancel is neat, clear and does not distract from or obliterate the underlying design of the stamp. It is legitimate and contemporaneous to the stamp. Serious collectors avoid favor cancels or contrived cancels, especially on expensive stamps—such as rare Washington-Franklin coil stamps—whose used value is either the same as or more than their unused value. Stamps whose used price closely approximates or exceeds their unused price are often seen with bogus cancels because clean used copies are more salable than no-gum or heavily hinged unused copies.

In many cases, the type of cancel on nineteenth century issues has a bearing on their value. Colored cancels, specialty cancels, and fancy cancels often add considerable premiums to the value of a stamp. Device-cancelled early stamps generally sell for more than pen-cancelled examples. Collectors avoid pen cancels on post-nineteenth century stamps. Refer to specialized catalogues for premiums and discounts for various types of cancels.

Cancelled to order (CTO) indicates that a cancellation was applied by the issuing government before the stamp was sold, often printed on entire sheets at the time of production. CTOs usually possess original gum despite being "used." CTOs are usually sold in bulk to packet and mixture makers. Serious collectors usually avoid CTOs.

Faults. Major faults include tears, thins, pinholes, creases, scuffs, abrasions, stains, foxing, discolorations, glazed gum, tropicalized gum, or anything else that might construed as damage. Minor or trivial faults include things such as perf bends and perf thins. As a general rule, the earlier the issue, the greater the percentage of its population that are faulty. The majority of expensive nineteenth century stamps contain faults.

Thins are usually the result of careless hinge removal and are visible from the back. Some creases are visible to the naked eye, others (such as ironed-out creases) are visible only in watermark fluid. Either way, they're considered faults. Fading, foxing, cellophane-tape staining, or any other discoloration puts a stamp in the faulty category. Faulty stamps are worth only a small fraction of catalogue value. The precise amount depends on the degree of the fault. Stamps with pieces missing are virtually worthless.

Other elements, such as straight-edges (collectors disdain straight edges on stamps that normally occur with perforations on all sides), heavy cancels, and poor centering, which technically are not faults, nevertheless, reduce the value of a stamp to a small fraction of catalogue value.

Natural inclusions (material embedded in paper during its manufacture), unnaturally irregular perfs, gum skips, perf dimples, toned paper, natural gum skips, and natural gum bends (unless severe enough to break the paper fibers), while not technically faults, are elements avoided by demanding buyers. The absence of these elements generally enhances the value of a stamp.

Unlike other collectible fields (such as fine art or antique automobiles) where restoration is accepted and encouraged, any attempt to improve the appearance of a stamp or repair it is generally regarded as tampering and is held in equally low esteem with outright fakery. Collectors have a strong and historical aversion to "improved" and repaired stamps, insisting instead on the best original condition. The standard for covers is not quite so strict. Erasure of pencil notations (if not evident) and other superficial improvements are generally not deemed improper.

Faulty stamps are often repaired by ironing out creases, bleaching discolorations, filling pinholes and thins, carefully coloring small scuffs and abrasions, and the like. Often, faults or repairs are not obvious, so it's wise to check carefully for any sign of tampering. Experienced buyers usually dip stamps face-down in watermark fluid to reveal creases, thins, closed tears, and repairs. They examine the face of a stamp, too, for any sign of tampering. Use a magnifying glass (a ten-power loupe works well and fits in pocket or purse) to examine stamps. Strong incandescent light works best, especially at stamp shows where lighting is often poor. Rotate the stamp and inspect it at different angles to better spot anomalies.

The presence of a major fault or repair generally diminishes the value of a stamp substantially, except in the case of extreme rarities that are not known (or seldom encountered) without faults or improvements. Many classic rarities were repaired years ago (closed tears glued shut, thins filled, etc.) and do not exist in an unaltered state.

"Improvements" such as regumming and reperforating fall into the same category as repairs. Regumming is a process intended to improve the appearance of a stamp by applying new gum to simulate original gum. Stamps—mostly nineteenth century issues, but some later issues as well—are most often regummed to replace unsightly disturbed gum or hinge remnants. Regummed stamps are typically offered as never-hinged, although some are occasionally lightly hinged in order to throw off suspicion that they have been regummed. All expensive nineteenth century stamps should be examined carefully for regumming.

Reperforating is a process of adding perforations to improve the appearance of a straight-edged stamp, or to improve centering by trimming a margin and adding perforations. As a result, many straight-edged copies—most often sheet margin copies—end up reperforated to simulate their more desirable, fully perforated counterparts.

Bear in mind that the vast majority of early stamps are faulty, repaired or "improved" and trade at a substantial discount from catalogue. The profusely illustrated book *How to Detect Damaged, Altered and Repaired Stamps,* by Paul Schmid, covers the subject in great detail. *Refer to the* Resource Guide.

Over the years, a number of attempts have been made to quantify the elements of condition and bring mathematical precision to grading, most often using computer analysis. Grade is largely a matter of subjective taste and in some cases even an acquired taste. It's impossible to reduce subjective visual esthetics to mathematics. There's just no objective way to measure "eye appeal." You might as well try to create a computer program to measure the physical beauty of human beings. As the old saying goes, "Beauty lies in the eye of the beholder," which is exactly why computer grading will never replace the human eye when it comes to stamp grading. The eye has been and will continue to be the best tool for grading stamps.

In summary, condition is the key factor of value. Sound stamps—those free of faults—are priced according to grade. Faulty stamps are worth only a small percentage of catalogue value—often as little as five percent to twenty percent. The grades of condition that might otherwise apply to a sound stamp, do not apply to a faulty stamp. Severely impaired stamps—such as those with pieces missing—are virtually worthless.

Experienced buyers look for premium quality stamps—stamps that exhibit the best qualities for their issue. In some cases, such as a perfectly centered, never-hinged, post-office-fresh $2.60 Zeppelin, it is easy to locate a premium copy. In others, such as an unused ten-cent 1847, it is almost impossible. So, maintain a sense of balance. Strive for quality but never let the quest for quality blind you to the limitations of an issue. Some buyers become so obsessed with quality that they begin to find something wrong with every stamp, regardless of its general excellence. Avoid unrealistic expectations and never forget the frailties and limitations of nineteenth century stamps. The rarer the stamp, the more difficult it will be to find in premium condition and the less picky one can afford to be. Some stamps are so rare that a reasonable population of candidates simply does not exist and selectivity, in the normal sense, is not possible.

Experienced, knowledgeable buyers recognize the genuine scarcity of premium quality stamps—especially nineteenth century issues—and are increasingly willing to pay double, triple, and even as much as ten times catalogue, for the truly one-in-a-thousand gem. The book *The Buyer's Guide: An Analysis of Selected U.S. Postage Stamps* offers an analysis of premium characteristics of U.S stamps on a stamp-by-stamp basis designed to help buyers know what to expect from each issue. *Refer to the* Resource Guide.

BUYING

The key to profit is buying as advantageously as possible. Stamps are available from many sources: retail dealers, mail order dealers, auctions, mail bid sales, stamp shows, clubs, classified advertisements, and increasingly, on the Internet.

Public Auction. If you're serious about stamp investing, you can't afford not to consider buying at public auction. Dealers pay attention to auction results to get a sense of the market and of prices in general.

If possible, attend an auction in person to get a feel for the action, the ebb and flow of bidding. Pay attention to who's bidding and on what. Are dealers ignoring material that has been previously "hot?" If so, perhaps the market for the item or specialty is cooling off. Are dealers bidding aggressively? Is the floor packed or sparse? Are the same few people doing all the bidding and buying? Each bidder is expressing an opinion about the market.

Inexperienced bidders often ask of a lot, "How much will it take to buy it?" Don't think that way. You'll end up stretching for lots, paying more than you should. The idea is to buy right, not to buy at any cost. You want only those lots you can secure advantageously. Figure out in advance at what price you cannot say "no" to a lot. That's your top bid. Stick to it. Never bid more. Don't get caught up in a bidding frenzy and overpay.

You'll lose more lots than you win using this strategy—and by a wide margin—but the good news is, you'll really make out on those you end up buying. At one recent auction, I bid on more than 400 lots, winning only ten—but I bought them right! Don't be discouraged if you miss out on a lot—there are always more. And if you have no luck at all, there are always more auctions. I realized years ago that there would always be more stamps than I would ever have money for. Keep that in mind and bid conservatively.

View lots in advance, if possible, so that you'll know exactly what you're getting. Some auctions are conservative in their descriptions, others are more zealous. You don't want any unpleasant surprises after the hammer drops because all sales are final.

Be aware that sometimes viewers disparage lots with comments such as "Looks regummed to me," in order to plant seeds of doubt and discourage others from bidding on them. And those who have doubts about their ability to spot regumming (or other problems) usually shy away from such lots. More often than not, you'll see the fellow who knocked the lot bidding on it. It's an old trick.

On the other hand, a faulty stamp occasionally sneaks by a lot describer. I hate to admit it, but there have been times when I was too busy to view lots, so I bid blind, surprised at the lack of competition, only to find out after I'd bought a lot that the reason no one else had bid on the lot was because it was faulty. Viewers have the edge over those who don't view because they have better information. So view each lot.

Sometimes a careless description works in your favor. I once picked up a collection at auction for $200 that contained a rare Washington-Franklin series coil line pair, which I subsequently consigned to another auction where it sold for more than $8,000. The rarity lay hidden in an album, hinged under a common coil pair of similar design. The album was described as a remainder—a term applied to albums and collections containing items whose individual value is too small to be lotted separately. It was a beat up old-time album containing scores of duplicate pairs hinged under one another, as was the custom years ago. The lot describer must have scanned the album briefly, noticed only inexpensive coil pairs, and assumed the ones mounted underneath were duplicates. The rare pair escaped the notice of bidders as well. I bought the lot quietly just at the estimated price, $200. So examine lots carefully.

Why don't the pros pick up on these opportunities? Often they do. I did. But just as often, they don't have time to view lots or they view them hurriedly. Remember, bidding at auction is usually more work for a dealer than fun. Something he's got to do to get inventory. At least in my case, it's often a grind, something I postpone until the last minute, and then spend time with a catalogue only because I have to. Dealers get dozens and dozens of catalogues, each with hundreds or thousands of lots. Before long the lots and descriptions begin to blur together and the stamps begin to look the same. The dealer's edge is sometimes offset by fatigue or inattentiveness.

Why don't collectors pick up on the misdescribed lots? Sometimes they do if the lot contains material of interest to them. But collectors tend not to be bargain hunters, at least not in the sense that they'll bid on anything if it's cheap enough. Mostly they're interested only in material that fits into their collection and tend to ignore everything else. And collectors tend not to be risk takers. They tend to lack confidence in their own expertise, reasoning that the pro—the lot describer—is unlikely to have made a mistake.

Look for material that's not in its best venue. For example, a stray U.S. Zeppelin set in an auction of specialized British Commonwealth. Lots like these tend to get lost in the shuffle and ignored by bidders who've come for the main event. They tend to sell for less than they would in a sale devoted to like material. Better still if they appear unobtrusively near the end of a long sale, when most of the enthusiasm and money have been spent and the floor is exhausted.

Look for sales with an overwhelming abundance of the same item. This would seem to contradict the previous advice, but notice that I said an abundance of the "same item," not "similar material." Successive lots of identical stamps tend to decrease in hammer price, and the more lots of the same item, the more the price tends to slip. Sometimes even three or four identical lots are enough to depress price. Generally, the first and last lots tend to sell for more than those in between. The fellow that's got to own it at any price generally buys the first lot. Other potential bidders usually sit out the intervening lots, reasoning that the last lot will be the cheapest. That's not always the case. Sometimes two like-minded bargain hunters end up duking it out over the last lot.

A few years back, I spotted a dozen identical airmail covers autographed by Charles Lindbergh buried in the back of a catalogue of a major New York auction. I knew the covers to be worth $1,000 to $1,250 each. They were completely out of place in the sale, which was devoted to classic U.S. stamps. The covers looked as if they had been added as an afterthought. The write-up was skimpy—the first cover minimally described, and each subsequent lot listed as "another similar lot." The describer must have been bone-tired and minutes before deadline when he wrote the descriptions. How utterly uninspiring and unappetizing the twelve lots sounded. No adjectives such as "fresh, rare, superb" to catch bidders' attention, just the bland "another similar lot," again and again. Only the first lot was illustrated, unobtrusively tucked toward the bottom corner of a page, overshadowed by a collage of other covers. I smelled an opportunity.

I gave my agent (more about agents later) a bid of $450 per lot. The first lot sold to the floor at one advance over my bid—$475. I bought the remaining 11 lots for an average price of $275 per lot. Altogether—with buyer's fee and agent commission—the purchase totaled $3,600. Within three months, I'd sold four of the covers for a total of $4,100. I had my money back and seven covers to hold at no cost. That's what I mean by buying smart—and this type of situation occurs time and time again.

External factors affect auctions and sometimes present opportunities. The unexpected blizzard that discourages attendance and reduces competition. The bad day on Wall Street or the international crisis that stifles bidding and depresses prices, if only temporarily. During the week after the stock market crash of October 1987, nervous bidders sat on the sidelines and much excellent material went begging. Two weeks later after everything had calmed down, they were back in force as if nothing had happened. In the meantime, there were bargains to be had. It takes nerve to buy in the face of unpleasant news, but some of the best opportunities ride on the coattails of bad news.

Summer is often a good time to buy and conversely, a poor time to sell. Years ago, the auction trade more or less shut down during the summer months because collectors were busy with vacations and outdoor activities. That changed during the boom years of the 1970s. Auctioneers held auctions as fast as material came in. After the boom ended, they continued to hold summer auctions, but they're usually not as strong as those held during the cold-weather months.

When bidding at auction, avoid going head to head with serious buyers. Instead, look for targets of opportunity and be ready to pounce. This requires self-discipline because in the heat of bidding the impulse is to run the race, outlast the competition, beat them at any cost, but that's exactly what you don't want to do. The idea is to get the lot at the minimum, not the maximum.

I like to sit toward the back of the room where I have a panoramic view of the action and where it's difficult for others to see how I'm bidding. I avoid jumping in at the beginning of bidding on a lot. Let the most anxious get their bids out of their system. When the flurry has died down and the auctioneer is about ready to hammer down the lot, I raise my paddle unobtrusively. Usually by that time, the impulse to race has passed. Bidders tend to lose heart more easily after the initial flurry of bidding has died. It doesn't happen every time, but often enough to pay off.

Bidders use all kinds of bidding techniques, such as jumping in early and aggressively to intimidate others. This tactic only makes sense if you intend to buy a lot at any price and have nothing to lose by gambling that you can frighten off the competition. It's not for bargain hunters.

I often use an auction agent when I can't attend an auction in person. I use an agent because I don't want to pay any more than I have to and in some cases, I need someone to view lots for me. Virtually all auctions take mail bids in addition to floor bids. Mail bids—when successful—are supposed to buy lots at one advance over the next highest bid. For example, if the top mail bid is $100 and the second high bid is $70—be it a floor bid or other mail bid—the lot should be sold for $80, or one advance over the second high bid of $70. Many—but not all—auctions follow this policy. Others do not. In some cases, you end up paying the full $100 regardless of what the second high bid was. I learned this the hard way years ago and that's why I started using an agent.

The very first time I used an agent, I bid $1,000 on a lot estimated at $500 to $750. It was a "must own" lot for my collection, not a buy-it-right investment purchase, but the result illustrates my point just the same. I won the lot for $300, plus $15 in agent fees, a fraction of what I had been willing to pay. Years later, when my collecting focus changed, I sold the stamp to a dealer for $750. I enjoyed it during the time I owned it, and it proved to be a good investment because I bought it right.

I do bid at some auctions by mail or fax without using an agent because I know from experience that my top bids will only be used if necessary. Unfortunately, the only way to sort out those who play fair from those who don't is through trial and error or through word of mouth. Most auction firms list the names of established auction agents in their auction catalogues.

An agent can do more than just save you money. Agents attend auctions week-in and week-out and have their hands on the pulse of the market. Feedback after a sale—who did most of the buying (collectors, dealers or other agents), what was hot, what was not—is valuable intelligence and can be worth its weight in gold. Some agents will keep their eyes open for the kind of material you're interested in and alert you when they spot it in an upcoming sale.

Agents typically charge from three to five percent of the total purchase price. Rates vary depending on size of account, frequency of bidding, and whether travel or viewing is involved. Most charge a minimum fee if none of a client's bids are successful.

Some auctions use reserves below which a lot will not sell. In some cases, every lot is reserved. In other cases, only a portion of the lots are reserved. The most straightforward list the minimum or reserve bids with the lot description. The others don't identify reserved lots and leave you to guess. Don't be induced to bid more than your instinct tells you just because a lot is reserved. The best auctions, in my opinion, are unreserved auctions. I prefer them because I think they offer the best opportunities.

Stamp Dealers. Having said that retail buying is poor investment strategy does not mean that you cannot or should not find investment material at retail stamp dealers. In fact, establishing a relationship with an experienced full-time professional is a great asset.

An active dealer is an excellent source for the kind of ear-to-the-ground information you need to stay on top of the stamp market and a great source for explaining the intricacies and subtleties of specialty material you may be considering for purchase. Few are better qualified to demonstrate how to spot fakes and altered stamps than professionals who handle stamps every day.

Look for dealers who have been around for a few years. Those who have stood the test of time have done so because they've treated their customers fairly. The longer a dealer has been in business, the greater his knowledge and experience. Remember, an opinion is only as good as the qualifications of the opinion giver. And several opinions are better than one.

An active dealer usually has a better sense of the market than a part-time dealer. Pay attention to what others, both collectors and dealers, think of him. Reputation is one of the best indicators of reliability. Many—but not all—dealers belong to the American Stamp Dealers Association (ASDA). ASDA dealers are required to have been in business at least a minimum number of years and they must provide credit and trade references before being accepted into membership. The ASDA also requires dealers to address and resolve complaints lodged against them or face expulsion, which offers consumers an extra layer of protection. Not all dealers are ASDA members. Many reliable dealers are not. The ASDA publication, "The Stamp Dealer's Obligations and Responsibilities When Selling Stamps as Investments," appears in the Appendix.

Some dealers tend to be conservative in grading, others push grades. Some dealers are low key in their sales approach, others are more aggressive. Some offer a return privilege, which is useful especially if you're new. Ten days or two weeks is pretty standard.

If a purchase is subject to certification, make sure the dealer notes that on your receipt. Stamp dealers are known for being generous with their knowledge, so ask questions. But bear in mind that the time to ask questions is before you make a purchase, not after. Ask for specific investment recommendations if you like, but bear in mind that it sets up a possible conflict of interest because almost certainly the recommendation will be for something that's in inventory rather than a completely objective opinion. In all likelihood the dealer will suggest something that he honestly believes is a good investment. Still, it's better to do your own homework, form your own opinions, and make decisions independent of the pressure to purchase a recommendation on the spot. Ask questions, gather information, select what you think holds promise, then locate it at the best price.

Sometimes the best price is from the dealer, especially if it's something outside his specialty. Let the dealer in U.S. stamps know that you're looking for Timbuktu. He's usually more than happy to sell to a ready customer than to have to ship the stamps and wait for his money. Sometimes you may be able to get it for the price he'd get shipping it to a specialist or, perhaps, a little more. Let him know that you expect to buy reasonably.

Don't ask a stamp dealer if the stamps you purchased elsewhere are a good deal. There is nothing he dislikes more. It puts him on the spot. Each time someone asks me that question, I cannot help but think, *if you were unsure about the price, why did you buy the stamps? You should have done your homework.* Dealers inevitably lose respect for those who pester them to validate purchases.

The more knowledge you acquire, the better your investment decisions will be. Ask questions and gather knowledge with an eye toward being able to rely on your own counsel to make investment choices.

Mail Order Dealers. When buying by mail, make sure the dealer has a return policy. Inspect stamps carefully on receipt to confirm identification and grading. Look for dealers with a reputation for conservative grading. Overgraded stamps are not bargains. Remember that grading is subjective and that even within a firm, two employees may see a stamp differently.

ASDA or APS (American Philatelic Society) membership offers mail order buyers an extra layer of protection because they follow up on consumer complaints.

Stamp Shows. There's no better venue for comparison shopping, networking and getting a feel for what's going on in the market. Walk the floor, peruse retail offerings, study the selection. Chat with dealers and meet collectors. Don't hesitate to ask questions. The more the better.

Take time to view the exhibits. Pay attention to how serious philatelists approach the hobby. Chat with exhibitors. They're usually more than happy to discuss their exhibits. Remember, the more you know, the greater your opportunities.

Individuals. I don't recommend buying from individuals unless you really know what you're doing, unless you're completely conversant with assessing condition, faults, and fakery. My experience has been that individual collectors are very forgiving when it comes to grading their own stamps, especially when selling. It's not intentional misrepresentation so much as functional blindness, the kind proud parents display when talking about their children.

I could write a whole book on horror stories arising from purchases made from individuals. The following two incidents are illustrative.

One of my customers—I'll call him Mr. Smith—bought $1,500 worth of magnificent never-hinged duck stamps from an individual he'd found in the classified section of the local newspaper. He didn't think it odd that the seller was from out of town. Or that he suggested they meet in a hotel lobby. Or that he insisted on being paid in cash. According to Smith, the seller turned out to be a personable old gentleman with a stockbook full of gorgeous stamps. Page after page of mouth-watering gems—Columbians, Zeppelins, and early duck stamps. Each perfect in every respect—wide margins, pristine gum and vivid color. Smith had never seen so many eye-popping stamps in one place before. And they were bargain priced.

"Why let a dealer horn in on the action?" the seller asked. "I'd rather see a fellow collector get a break. And by the way, another gentleman is coming by later this afternoon, so you'd be wise to take what you want now."

Smith couldn't resist. He plucked one gem after another from the stockbook—$1,500 worth of the choicest items. He counted out fifteen one-hundred dollar bills, thanked the old gentleman, and headed home to savor his good fortune.

Weeks passed. He studied the stamps more closely and began to have doubts. Finally, he asked my opinion.

"They're either regummed or reperfed, aren't they?" he said as I looked over the stamps.

"Yes," I said, "They are."

"Every single one?"

"Every single one . . . and beautiful work. Tremendous craftsmanship."

"I should have known better," he sighed. "But he seemed like such a nice old guy. I feel like a fool."

Smith should not have allowed his awe to override his prudence. Professionals don't. The first thing they do is look for faults and evidence of tampering. This from bitter experience—dealers think of it as paying their dues. And pros learn to ignore a seller's comments. Too many sad stamps are accompanied by the most wonderful patter. Stamps must stand on their own merits. Pros never let anything distract them from an objective assessment.

The second incident truly drives home the point that the buyer must beware. I had a feeling the first time Mr. Jones called that things weren't going to work out right, but I went to his house anyway, lured by his smooth talk and by the promise that the collection he'd inherited was large and valuable. He'd persuaded me to waive my appraisal fee, assuring me that he was ready to sell if I'd just come out and make an offer. So I went. The collection sounded too good to pass up.

It was voluminous—stockbooks, mint sheet files, albums, cartons full of material. As I worked my way through it, Jones entertained me with tales of his business prowess—how he'd gotten the best of so-and-so in a real estate deal, how he'd gotten the inside track on a beverage distributorship, how his idiot brother-in-law wouldn't have lasted two weeks in business had it not for his generosity, and so on. He enjoyed spinning the tales, chuckling as he told them.

I'd been working a couple of hours when his wife came into the room to tell him she'd be gone the rest of the day. They could discuss my offer when she returned that evening, she said.

"I thought you were ready to do business on the spot," I said after she'd left.

"I am . . . but you can't very well expect me to take your offer without running it by my wife," he hedged.

There would be no deal that day, I realized. No matter how much I offered.

"I'll flip through the rest of the collection and give you a general range of value. If you decide it's in the ballpark, I'll come back and figure everything to the last penny."

"Fine," Jones said

I riffled the remaining albums, stockbooks, and boxes.

"Looks like somewhere between ten and twenty thousand dollars," I said. As near as I could tell from my quick perusal the collection was worth about $15,000, but I wanted to allow myself a little leeway. I was sure Jones would use my figure to fish for a better offer, and I didn't want to get bumped by a couple of hundred bucks. I left with the empty feeling that he was playing me like one of those guys he had boasted about getting the better of.

Time passed. I didn't hear a word from him.   At a stamp show several months later, the dealer across the aisle from my booth mentioned that he was going out to look at a big collection that evening. He didn't elaborate, so I didn't think much of it.

"How'd it go?" I asked the next morning.

"Beautiful collection, but the guy wanted way too much for it."

From his description of the stamps, I was sure it was the Jones collection.

"How much did he want, if you don't mind my asking?" I said.

"Twenty-five thousand."

I couldn't believe my ears.

"I figured it was worth about fourteen or fifteen thousand, maybe a bit more," the dealer said. "But twenty-five grand, no way."

During the ensuing conversation, I realized that although we were talking about the Jones collection, he had not been dealing with Jones.

"Where did your guy get the collection?" I asked.

"Bought it from a friend who'd inherited it. Got a deal, too. At least that's what he thought. Said his friend had a dealer come out and look it over. Said the dealer offered twenty thousand. If a dealer offers twenty thousand, he told his friend, you know it's got to be worth a lot more. And that poor guy bought it—hook, line, and sinker."

"I'm the dealer who looked at the collection!" I said. "I didn't offer twenty thousand. I told him it looked like it would be worth somewhere between ten and twenty thousand."

"Well, that may be, but his buddy Jones buried him in it. When I offered fourteen, he just about hit the roof. Said he'd paid twenty, and it ought to be worth at least twenty-five—easily."

Later that morning the owner of the collection showed up and prowled the aisles trying to line up dealers to come out to his house to make an offer. A couple did, but no one bought the collection. It wasn't worth what he wanted. By the end of the show it must have dawned on him that he'd been had.

The moral is, you'd better know your stuff when buying from an individual because unlike buying from a professional, you have no recourse.

Publicly Traded Stamp Funds. At this writing, no publicly traded stamp funds exist. A few years ago a major New York brokerage firm got its feet wet with a publicly offered rare coin fund. Unfortunately, it didn't work out well for either investors or the brokerage firm. The coins were too esoteric, acquired at inflated prices, and somewhat illiquid. The fund involved only a few million dollars, so it turned out to be more of an embarrassment than a financial catastrophe for the brokerage firm. But it demonstrated the perils of treating collectibles like financial investments. The brokerage house took its licks and went about its business as if nothing had happened. After that affair, don't look for any other collectible funds to be offered by Wall Street anytime soon.

Private Syndicates. Private syndicates are also known as pools, joint ventures or limited partnerships. Syndicates most often consist of a few individuals, anywhere from three or four to a dozen or more, each typically contributing $5,000 to $25,000. Investors often know one another or at least know the managing partner.

If you're inclined to seek out this type of situation, make sure that the managing partner is knowledgeable, reliable and experienced, someone with a proven track record, someone willing to put his own money at risk. If the managing partner is unwilling to risk any of his own cash, think twice about investing. At least, that's my opinion.

The syndicate's investment strategy should be clearly spelled out in advance—the kind of material that will be bought; the length of time it will be held; under what conditions it will be liquidated; how profits will be divided; and so forth. Get everything in writing and have a lawyer look it over before signing. And make sure that no conflicts of interest exist, such as the managing partner selling his own material to the syndicate.

Syndicates are not generally publicly marketed. They're usually well-kept secrets, like those unspoiled, off-the-beaten-path resorts on the Mexican gulf coast. Because syndicates are not subject to SEC oversight or regulation, it's best to know the managing partner before getting involved. Again, the invariable key to success is a reliable, knowledgeable, experienced managing partner—someone who knows the ropes.

Mass-Marketed Collectibles. Avoid mass-marketed stamps (or covers) for investment, the kind offered by direct mail or that appear in the Sunday newspaper supplements. The kind liberally laced with seductive buzz words, such as "limited edition" and "heirloom quality," intended to evoke an expectation of future appreciation without coming right out and saying, "Buy these.

They're a good investment." Although colorful and topically appealing (subjects include film stars, rock-and-roll legends, cartoon characters, and sadly, even the late Princess Diana), they offer almost no opportunity for profit. They're poor investments because there is almost no aftermarket for them.

They're typically "issued" by countries few have ever heard of, usually by special arrangement between the mass marketer and the country's postal administration. Many never appear on sale in the countries they purport to originate from. Draw a distinction between that which is issued primarily to serve a postal need and that which is issued primarily as a souvenir. Whether or not the "stamps" are "authorized" or "valid for postage" is merely splitting hairs and the buyer should look beyond the letter of the definition to the actual intent of the issue.

Avoid investing in mass-marketed philatelic products (typically series of stamps, first day covers, special event covers, and the like) through continuity (monthly installment) programs. At first blush, spending $15 or $20 a month would seem an economical way to accumulate valuable stamps and covers over a period of time. Unfortunately, investors rarely recapture more than a small fraction of the original price when selling. Again, because there is little aftermarket.

Should collectors be able to buy these kinds of stamps? Of course. After all, it's a free country. And there's no denying that they're pretty. Should they be marketed as investments? No, they should not. Buy them if you enjoy the visual esthetics, but don't expect to make a profit.

Portfolio-of-the-Month Programs. Generally, avoid investing in stamps on a portfolio-of-the-month basis. My experience has been that portfolio-of-the-month programs are more often oriented toward selling you stamps rather than making you money. I hate to sound so harsh but portfolio selections are more often a function of what's available in sufficient quantity to service subscribers than a function of what's likely to show the best price appreciation.

The Great Boom spawned dozens of portfolio-of-the-month services, each touting stamps as investments with slick brochures, which after a while began to sound as if they had been written by the same person. After the market softened in the early 1980s, most of the services vanished as quickly as they had appeared. For the most part, they were opportunists attracted by a hot market—as opportunists are attracted to all hot markets—whose convincing sales pitches appealed to those possessing little knowledge and little inclination to get any. They appealed to those who just wanted to get in on the easy money. Most of those operating the services had not been full-time stamp dealers before the boom and most left the trade after the boom. And those who wanted to get in on the easy money were disappointed.

Buying is the key to profit. This cannot be emphasized enough. In the final analysis, buying right is the key to profit. Avoid full retail except where an item appears underpriced by the market. Keep your eyes open for undervalued items.

SELLING

When to sell? Sell when you can take a profit and when you deem the potential for additional appreciation to be exhausted or so small that a better return could be found elsewhere.

Investments typically go through a dynamic phase, followed by a downward phase and then a static phase. Those who chart price behavior tell us that after a price peaks, the steepness of its downward trendline often mirrors the steepness of its ascending line. In other words, the faster something goes up, the faster it comes down. The idea is to sell at or before the peak, not on the way down.

A static phase often follows the downward phase, price neither rising nor falling but remaining steady—a flat horizontal line on a graph. This was the case with the stamp market in the mid-1980s after the gains run up in the boom evaporated.

Sometimes the static phase directly follows a run up. This is often the case with individual stamps or hot trends. Sometimes a hot stamp rises from $5 to $20 in six months, then remains at $20 for a decade. The reason is that collectors are reluctant to dump speculations. They hang on because they're comfortable owning the stamps and don't care if they continue to rise in price. They reason that they've made a profit so it doesn't cost anything to hold. They also often reason that since the item rose sharply once, it may do so again. From an investment standpoint, it doesn't make sense to hang on to an item once it has outrun its potential.

Cash out and move on to the next item. It's better to take your money and put it to work somewhere else.

Where to sell? Where you can get the most, of course. And that depends on what you have and how quickly you want your money. Liquidity is the speed with which an asset can be converted into cash. Stamps are not as liquid as some assets such as stocks and bonds but are more liquid than others such as real estate and fine art. Liquidity has a price, which is to say the faster you want your money, the less you get.

Let's examine the options.

Outright Sale. Outright sale is the simplest and most direct way to dispose of stamps. Once a price is agreed upon, settlement is immediate. You walk away with cash in hand. Outright sale usually means selling to a dealer.

Most dealers in America handle U.S. stamps. A specialist is usually the best market for other types of stamps. The dealer in error stamps usually pays the best price for error stamps. The same holds true for British Commonwealth stamps, Asian stamps, German stamps, and so forth.

Philatelic periodicals are loaded with advertisements of specialists. In addition, the two major stamp weeklies, *Linn's Stamp News* and *Stamp Collector*, publish directories of dealers listed by specialty. The ASDA publishes an annual directory of members cross referenced by specialty and geographic location. *Refer to the* Resource Guide

From the moment you acquire an investment, you should start thinking about where to sell it when the time comes. That means paying attention to who's dealing in what, who's buying what, and how much they're paying. Again, philatelic periodicals are a good place to start.

Years ago, I methodically sent selections of stamps to out-of-town dealers advertising to buy just to weed out the ones I wouldn't want to do business with when the time came to sell something significant. The exercise proved instructive. Some who advertised they paid top prices nit-picked my stamps in an attempt to knock the prices below their published offers. Some cherry picked what I'd sent, keeping the superb items and returning the rest. Some stalled on payment. But the best, didn't argue, didn't chisel, didn't cherry pick. They sent checks immediately and proved to be a pleasure to do business with. So, take time to check potential outlets for your stamps.

Almost any dealer in America can handle a modest holding of $5,000 or less. Consider a large dealer in a major city if you have stamps valued at $10,000 or more. Consider a major national firm, such as those in New York, Chicago, or Los Angeles, if your stamps are worth $50,000 or more.

Bear in mind that all stamp dealers are not the same. They buy according to their individual needs, perceptions and bankrolls. Generally the more active a dealer, the more likely he is to pay a competitive price. Dealers can't call up the factory to order more stamps. They have to buy from the public and that means being competitive. Usually the more desirable an item, the higher the percentage of catalogue (and retail) a dealer will pay. And the greater the value of your portfolio, the greater your options.

Avoid retail-sale consignment arrangements, despite the prospect of a higher return. Dealers who push this type of arrangement are often undercapitalized, the process ends up taking months, and only the best items sell. The potential problems associated with retail-sale consignment are not worth the hypothetical greater return.

As a general rule, don't sell the best items from a collection separately. Sell intact. Once the key pieces are gone, dealers won't be motivated to offer much for the balance.

Public Auction. Public auction offers an excellent opportunity to get the best price, if you have the right stamps. Auctions offer sellers direct access to that market, bringing stamps directly to interested, qualified buyers who bid competitively for the right to own them. Presumably when the hammer falls, everyone interested in your stamps will have bid on them and they will have sold to the highest bidder.

Auction is not right for every stamp. It won't work magic on common, low-priced stamps, won't turn junk into gold. High quality stamps do the best at auction, as do rarities and specialty items. Genuinely rare stamps—the kind that come to market only infrequently—often bring record prices at auction, as do lower priced stamps of superlative quality.

Some argue that the auction market is a wholesale market, and in many respects it is, but not entirely. In reality, the stamps that appeal to collectors—specialty material, material rarely offered on the market, material in superlative condition—are readily purchased by the end consumer—the collector.

Most auctions have consignment minimums, typically $1,000 net yield, although it varies from firm to firm. Narrow profit margins make it uneconomical to handle small consignments. If your consignment doesn't meet the minimum, chances are that it wouldn't do well at auction anyway.

Sellers usually pay a ten-percent commission, although some auctions have a sliding scale. Generally, the smaller the consignment and the smaller the value of the individual lot, the higher the commission. Some auctions charge a minimum fee per lot for lots that sell for less than $100. The fee is usually $10 or $15. If your consignment is large enough, you may be able to negotiate a fee.

First-class auction firms carefully describe and illustrate most lots in eye-appealing catalogues, which are mailed to customer lists often containing thousands of names, many of whom bid by mail.

Each consignment is lotted (subdivided into individual lots for auction) according to its merits. Stamps of substantial value or superlative quality are described and illustrated separately. The costs of lotting, catalogue printing and mailing, and overhead make it uneconomical to lot individual stamps whose value is less than $100. Stamps not meeting the individual lot minimum are grouped into lots commonly referred to as remainders or balances; however, stamps belonging to different consignors are never commingled.

Most auctions offer cash advances, typically 50 percent of the expected net yield, but sometimes more depending on how large and desirable the consignment is. Some charge interest on advances, others do not. Some add a percentage point or two to the commission in lieu of interest. An advance enables the seller to have some immediate cash, while at the same time affording the opportunity to realize a yield greater than might be obtained from outright sale.

Reputable auction firms give realistic estimates of expected net yields. This is important because you don't want any surprises later. Be suspicious of anyone who promises an unrealistically high yield to secure your consignment. You'll likely be disappointed after the sale.

Many consignors, especially inexperienced ones, request reserves (the minimum price below which a lot will not be sold) because they fear that their stamps might sell too cheaply. Some auction firms allow reserves, others do not. The fact is that lots with unrealistic reserves simply fail to attract bids. So unless you're willing to get stamps back and waste months going through the consignment pipeline a second time, forget about reserves.

My strategy is to consign enough material so that the yield averages out. As long as you're satisfied with the aggregate net yield quoted in the estimate (which is why it is so important to get a *realistic* estimate), don't waste time worrying about the price of each individual lot. Some lots sell for more than expected and others for less, but they tend to average out. Concern yourself with the estimated aggregate net yield and don't worry about individual lots. If you don't like the size of the estimate, don't consign.

Auctions that allow reserves usually charge for them. Others simply advise you to bid on your own lots if you want to protect them, in which cases, you're usually charged at least the seller's commission (10 percent) for lots you buy back, and in some instances, the buyer's premium (10 to 15 percent) as well. This cuts into profits. Occasionally, you hear horror stories about consignments with unrealistic reserves that end up almost completely unsold, costing consignors thousands of dollars in commissions.

The practice of charging for reserves is not unreasonable. Auctions put in the same amount of work and incur the same expenses whether a lot sells or not. They can't afford to hold sales and not sell lots.

Occasionally—but not often—an auction will agree to a no-fee, blanket reserve. Typically, those operations are new to the business or desperate for material. The reserves, an incentive to attract consignors, usually turn out to be an exercise in futility for both seller and auction alike. Their customer lists are usually not sufficiently developed to generate the kind of high-dollar bids necessary for the strategy to succeed. So the seller gets back most of his material and the auction loses the cost of offering the lots. Established auctions do not encourage reserves because, more often than not, those who insist on them have unrealistically high opinions of their stamps' value.

Seek out an auction firm with an established clientele for the type of material you have to offer. You won't get the best price for classic U.S. stamps, proofs and essays, or major errors through an auction firm that specializes in British Commonwealth. Large auction houses do best with expensive, high-profile material.

Small specialized auctions often get the strongest prices for material in their specialty. I once received $1,100 for a small box of World War II V-mail that I had consigned to small auction specializing in military postal history. I had picked the box up several years earlier at a stamp show for $75. I never found any retail customers for it and the best offer I could get from another dealer was $100, so it sat on the shelf until I discovered the specialist auction. I'd hoped to get about $150 and was flabbergasted when the lot sold for $1,100. So do your homework and sell in the right venue.

Obtain sample catalogues and prices realized for several recent sales in order to get an idea of how your stamps will be presented and how much similar stamps have realized. Try to get a commitment in advance about how your material will be lotted and presented. Ideally, stamps should be lotted individually (groupings tend to sell to dealers) and illustrated. Illustrated lots fetch higher prices than those not illustrated. If possible, speak to former consignors to find out if they were satisfied or dissatisfied. Read lot descriptions to get an idea of how your stamps will be described. Some firms tend toward descriptive minimalism, listing just the bare essentials, while others are more liberal and sales-oriented in their descriptions.

Consign stamps in a timely fashion. Don't wait until the last minute. Lot describers are under a lot of pressure at deadline precisely because consignors tend to procrastinate. Your stamps will usually get more careful attention if consigned early.

Experienced consignors prefer to have their material appear in fall or winter auctions, when the collecting season is in full swing. Sale by auction has some drawbacks. The results are not immediate. Typical time from consignment to settlement is four to six months. Settlement is usually made 30 to 45 days after the sale. Another drawback is that consignors assume market risk. In the time between consignment and sale, market prices can rise or fall. Drastic fluctuations rarely occur, still the element of uncertainty exists. And as mentioned earlier, unforseen occurrences such as a stock market crash affects confidence and prices.

Successful bidders are normally permitted to have stamps expertized if they so desire. Payments for lots submitted for expertizing are not dispersed to consignors until the lots have been returned with good expert certificates. Established auction firms usually correctly identify stamps when lotting, so the risk of having a stamp that's been submitted for expertizing returned is small. Still, the time involved delays payment. Some consignors prefer to have stamps expertized before consigning because bidders tend to bid more liberally on expertized lots.

Foreign auctions can be useful for the right property. It is axiomatic that stamps are most in demand in the nation of their origin. German and Swiss auctions advertise heavily in the United States for consignments. Some Swiss auctions even offer to deposit proceeds directly into a Swiss back account opened in the consignor's name. Foreign auctions often get tremendous prices for top-quality, specialized material native to their locale, but they tend to be very selective. Unless you have a specialized, high-dollar property, a foreign auction probably won't be interested in your consignment.

When consigning abroad, go in with your eyes open—terms and conditions vary from nation to nation. Some foreign auctions charge lotting and illustration fees (most U.S. auctions don't). You may encounter insurance fees, special taxes, and other types of fees typically not encountered in U.S. auctions. Also, remember that in case of disagreement, your stamps are outside United States jurisdiction and beyond easy legal recourse.

Some foreign auctions have the annoying habit of reserving lots whether you want reserves or not. It's very frustrating to wait six months for your stamps to be sold, only to receive most of them back. It's happened to me and I didn't like it. And one more thing, don't consign U.S. stamps to foreign auctions. The best market for U.S. stamps is in the United States.

Private Treaty. Private treaty is best for collections or individual items of significant value. In a private treaty arrangement the dealer acts as a broker, taking a commission, which is usually negotiated. Ask the dealer for an estimate of how quickly the stamps will sell. Agree on a time limit. Thirty days is usually sufficient unless the property requires special presentation such as a printed brochure. Often, the dealer can arrange a sale quickly with a few phone calls or a special mailing—sometimes within a few days or weeks.

Listen to the dealer's advice on pricing, but be aware that dealers sometimes suggest a price toward the lower end of the expected range in order to move the goods quickly. Sellers tend to lean toward the high end. The high end makes more sense if the market is hot, either in general or for the specific items.

Make sure terms of payment are understood by both parties. Avoid time payments unless you don't mind them. Make sure the dealer retains possession of the stamps until payment from the buyer is received. Get everything in writing and make sure you have photocopies of your stamps.

Direct Sale to Other Collectors. It's usually more trouble than it's worth. Collectors tend to pick and choose rather than buy an entire holding, even if it's priced right. Some subsequently get buyer's remorse. Occasionally a check will bounce. And if you're considering advertising in the daily paper, remember that crooks read classified ads, too.

Stamp Exchanges. Several attempts have been made to establish stamp exchanges that would operate in a fashion similar to the New York Stock Exchange. The most ambitious attempt in the mid-1980s envisioned collectors, investors, and institutions making trades through a series of members, floor brokers, and member brokers for modest commissions. The exchange failed to generate enough volume to make narrow commissions profitable, perhaps because stamps (especially large-dollar transactions) do not lend themselves to sight-unseen trading.

Internet. The Internet has opened up the possibility of buying, selling, and trading directly with other individual collectors all over the world. Much of the action takes place on online auctions, which are springing up all over. They fall into two categories: party-to-party auctions and traditional auctions. Party-to-party auction sites act at arm's length, offering a forum in which buyer and seller interact directly. Ebay (*www.ebay.com*) is one of the largest, although not devoted exclusively to stamps. Others exist and can be located using a search engine. Online auctions are easy to use and commissions are small. Inexpensive stamps tend to sell well; however, at this writing, there is still some reluctance among buyers to bid top prices for sight-unseen stamps offered by unknown individuals. We say "sight-unseen" even if a lot is illustrated by a scanned image because a scanned image does not permit the type of critical close-up inspection necessary to reveal faults and make a complete condition and grade assessment.

Increasingly, traditional auctions are coming online. They differ from party-to-party auctions in that they actually receive the stamps to be sold, examine them, and verify them. Knowing that lots are accurately described and graded (especially by an established auction) gives bidders the confidence to bid freely. This is vital to a getting the best price, especially for a expensive stamps.

The subject of selling is more completely covered in the book *Top Dollar Paid!, The Complete Guide to Selling Your Stamps.* *Refer to the* Resource Guide.

OPPORTUNITIES

The key to success in investment is to anticipate demand, take a position, then sell into a rising market. In order to do that, develop an eye for quality and a nose for opportunity.

Learn to recognize opportunities, whether a broad bull market, an emerging trend, or a single item. Bull markets come along only infrequently. Trends appear all the time. Some trends are broad in scope, such as stamps of the Far East, others are more narrow, such as plate number coils (PNCs) or error stamps. Some last longer than others, but all tend to brighten, shine, then fade.

The following are not recommendations, but interesting possibilities. Remember, the purpose of this book is to teach you how to think and analyze, not tout. So, consider the following instructive for the reasoning and decide for yourself if they have merit.

Gem Quality. Years ago—back in the 1950s—coin collectors graded coins into several broad categories—good, fine, extremely fine, about uncirculated, uncirculated and gem uncirculated. Collectors weren't too fussy, descriptions were pretty relaxed. But over time, the market became more quality conscious, especially as prices rose. In response to this, the hobby developed a precise numerical grading scale with seventy increments. Coins were described using specific numerical grades such as AU-55 (about uncirculated) or MS-60 (uncirculated) rather than informal terminology. Mint state (MS) grades referred to uncirculated coins,

MS-60 being the lowest uncirculated grade, with each numerical grade above MS-60 describing an increasingly pristine state of condition.

As grades became more precisely defined, price differences between them widened. In the old days, an uncirculated coin worth $100 usually fetched a small premium—perhaps 10 or 20 percent—if it was unusually nice. After numerical grading, price differences for each grade above MS-60 widened. Compare the prices (as of this writing) for various grades of a common-date, $10 Indian gold piece: MS-60, $365; MS-63, $700; MS-64, $1,350; and MS-65, $4,800. The reason for the startling disparity in prices is that truly perfect coins are extremely difficult to find.

Awareness of the rarity of truly gem-quality examples of early mint stamps has not completely dawned on the stamp market yet, but it is only a matter of time. The invariable trend in all collecting fields is toward ever-increasing quality consciousness and finer shadings of grades.

Back in the 1950s, stamps fell into three broad categories: well-centered, poorly centered, and seconds. Seconds were either faulty, heavily cancelled, or impaired in some other way. No one paid much attention to hinging. Over the years, attitudes changed. Hinging became an important—if not the most important—single attribute of condition. Collectors also began to pay more attention to centering and the size of margins. Grading standards tightened and became more refined, especially during the Great Boom, when buyers demanded the highest quality, and dealers—aware of the scarcity of premium quality stamps—began charging accordingly. And the trend toward increased quality consciousness continues.

In the beginning, collectors focused on completion. Now that completion is not a realistic goal for most collectors, the emphasis has shifted to quality.

As mentioned earlier, the majority of expensive nineteenth century stamps are faulty, and of the sound stamps, the majority are off-quality. Gem copies are few and far between.

Right now the spread in prices seems to be greater at the low end of the spectrum than at the premium end. For example, using a numerical scale where 100 percent represents catalogue price, faulty copies are worth about 10 percent; average copies (sound but visually unappealing), about 20 percent; fine copies, about 35-50 percent; fine-to-very-fine copies, about 75 percent; very fine copies, 100 percent; extremely fine copies, about 150 percent; and gem superb (OG, NH, fresh, jumbo) copies, about 150 to 500 percent. The spread in prices between very fine copies and gem superb copies ranges from about 150 to 500 percent. Compare that with the spread between MS-60 and MS-65 grades in the earlier example of the gold coin. The highest grades of stamps may be underpriced. It is reminiscent of the days when gem quality uncirculated coins sold for only slightly more than run-of-the-mill uncirculated coins.

And consider the following mint U.S. stamps, which are priced in very fine condition in one of the major stamp catalogues. The $5 Columbian of 1893 is priced at $3,500 hinged and $5,500 never-hinged (a 57-percent NH premium). The 50-cent Columbian of the same series is priced at $550 hinged and $800 never-hinged (a 45-percent NH premium). And the $2.60 Zeppelin of 1930 is priced at $850 hinged and $1,200 never-hinged (a 41-percent premium). The premiums for the three stamps are in the same ballpark, but the number of never-hinged stamps for each is not.

According to a survey of more than 100,000 scarce stamps that appeared at auction (source: *The Buyers Guide, An Analysis of Selected U.S. Postage Stamps*), only one in two hundred $5 Columbians are never-hinged. One in nine 50-cent Columbians are never-hinged. The $5 Columbian is twenty-two times scarcer than the 50-cent Columbian never-hinged, yet the premium is only slightly more.

One of every two $2.60 Zeppelins is never-hinged. Never-hinged $5 Columbians are 100 times scarcer never-hinged than never-hinged $2.60 Zeppelins, yet the never-hinged premium for the $5 Columbian is only slightly more than for the $2.60 Zeppelin. Never-hinged $5 Columbians would appear to be woefully undervalued. Could it be that superlative quality U.S. stamps are inexpensive in relation to their true scarcity? If that's the case, perhaps an opportunity exists to pick up super select grades at prices that may later look like bargains.

Remember that historically the trend has been toward more sophisticated grading and greater price spreads between grades.

And the supply of gem-quality rare stamps is so limited that any increase in demand should exert significant pressure on price.

Most catalogues reflect prices in only a couple of grades, applying the same premium for truly rare, premium-quality stamps to those that are not. Opportunities exist at present to purchase stamps that are truly scarce in premium-quality condition for reasonable prices.

Definitives. Serious philatelists tend to look down on "philatelic" covers, that is covers created by someone with philatelic knowledge or for a philatelic purpose. Commemorative stamps could almost be regarded as "philatelic" in the sense that they are created specifically for stamp collectors.

Traditionally, definitive stamps have been the workhorse stamps, performing day-to-day service rather than a philatelic purpose. Increasingly, serious collectors are forming specialized collections of definitives because fewer face-different stamps are issued, because defintives are more economical to collect, and because they are bored with just filling spaces.

Over the years, new-issue hoarders tended to ignore definitives because they were available for extended periods of time (usually 10 to 15 years) and because they were not perceived as being scarce or desirable. Because so few (in comparison to commemoratives) were saved, they're usually worth more than commemoratives of the same era. This is true for definitives of foreign countries as well. Definitive sets and covers (especially those containing high values or esoteric uses) have been rising in price much faster than their commemorative counterparts.

There's a definitive series to fit every budget, from early classics to modern issues.

Specialized Collections. Collectors have shifted their attention away from completion to narrower goals, most often either topical collections or specialized collections. Specialized collections offer the opportunity not only to collect, but to build a property that is larger than the sum of its parts. Specialized collections invariably attract much attention and spirited bidding when they appear at auction, regardless of whether they are multi-million-dollar holdings such as the *Honolulu Advertiser* collection of Hawaiian stamps or more modest holdings, such as the Liberty definitive series.

Collections of modern definitives are growing in popularity, even collections of single denominations. One fellow spent years accumulating modern certified mail covers, most of which he spent less than a quarter apiece for, only to get an average of several dollars per cover when he sold the collection. It didn't make him wealthy, but his rate of return was astronomical. There's a specialty for every budget.

Specialist collectors, because of their narrow focus, are usually able to buy more intelligently, to spot bargains that are not apparent to the less knowledgeable. In the process, they can build valuable collections that are in demand the moment they are brought to market. Remember, dealers and collectors alike have an eye for the unusual, for that which is not encountered every day.

Germany.   With few exceptions, the essential market for stamps is in the nation of their origin. Prices for German stamps are established in Germany; British stamps, in Great Britain; and so forth. Generally, the more broadly based and affluent a market, the more opportunity for price appreciation.

Germany has been and continues to be a philatelic powerhouse. It has a large, active and organized body of stamp collectors and a large dealer network—more than 800 strong according to the German stamp dealers' association, the *Bundesverband des Deutschen Briefmarkenhandels*. What makes Germany interesting to the investor is its history of political turmoil. First the Nazis, then the division into East and West Germany and the city-state of West Berlin (all of which issued their own postage stamps), and finally reunification.

During the Cold War, East Germans pursued stamp collecting avidly, but were prohibited from owning anything relating to the Nazi regime, including stamps. Since reunification, prices of Third Reich issues have increased steadily—if not dramatically—as former East Germans try to fill in the missing years, 1933-1945, in their albums. Sets of Third Reich stamps that could be had for a dollar or two only a few years ago now command $10, $20, even

$30 a set, and prices have been rising all across the spectrum. As former East Germans become more affluent, prices for the once forbidden material should continue to rise. After all, we're talking about a lot of empty album spaces.

And there are other interesting possibilities in the German area for those with the patience to ferret them out.

The Far East. The burgeoning economies of the Far East offer interesting opportunities. Hong Kong is a hotbed of philatelic activity, not only for issues of Hong Kong, but for stamps of China as well. Stamps of Hong Kong are also in demand in America and among collectors of British Commonwealth.

Stamp collecting is also enormously popular in the People's Republic of China. Beijing boasts two large outdoor stamp markets, which between them contain somewhere between 300 and 500 dealers. As the vast population of China becomes more affluent, they will almost certainly spend more money on stamps. New affluent Chinese already invest in stamps as a hedge and because they are wary of keeping too much money in banks.

During the cultural revolution of the late 1960s, China issued a variety of colorful, propaganda-related stamps featuring Chairman Mao, slogans of the cultural revolution, and joyful workers holding high the red banner of communism. Ironically, at the same time, Chinese authorities actively discouraged stamp collecting, calling it bourgeois. So, few dared save these colorful stamps, and few of these stamps found their way overseas. Stamps issued during the cultural revolution routinely cost as much as $10, $20 or $30 *per stamp*, and many sell for much more—hundreds of dollars. By comparison, the majority of U.S. commemorative stamps of the same era cost less than a quarter apiece. A word of caution, though, beware of fakes.

Stamps of other nations of the Far East such as Korea, Singapore, and Taiwan, also merit investigation. There appears to be much room for growth.

Duck Stamps. Duck stamps are issued by the Department of the Interior for use by waterfowl hunters on hunting licenses. They're expensive in relation to postage stamps (at this writing $15 face value per stamp) and therefore not typically purchased in multiples by collectors. The factors that make duck stamps interesting are, (1) they appeal to three types of collectors—stamp collectors, hunters, and conservationists; (2) their high face value discourages new-issue hoarding and implies a thin, well distributed supply; (3) pre-1970 duck stamps appear on dealer buy lists week-in and week-out. In addition, duck stamps are visually appealing, a factor one should never underestimate.

Consider mint, never-hinged, pre-1970 issues when they can be picked up reasonably.

Contrarian Opportunities. In the late 1970s I bought a carton of Vietnam-related material from a local stamp dealer. It was a hodge-podge accumulated by a former serviceman while on active duty in Vietnam. The carton contained lots of covers, especially with ancillary markings such as "Killed in Action," etc. It also contained several $1 Airlift stamps on wrappers. The $1 Airlift stamp was issued in 1968 for use on parcels sent to servicemen overseas. They're quite common unused, but rarely seen on cover or wrapper used for their intended purpose.

At the time, the bad taste of the war still lingered and no one wanted anything to do with Vietnamese stamps or anything war related. The carton looked like a bunch of junk, but I had a hunch that sooner or later former servicemen would become interested in postal history relating to the Vietnam war. In addition, I'd never come across an accumulation of similar material, so I reasoned that it must be scarce.

I bought the carton for $100, which seemed like a big price at the time, and stuck it on a back shelf. A few years later I noticed a display of military mail similar to that in the carton at a dealer's booth at a Denver stamp show. I mentioned the carton to the dealer.

"Why don't you bring it in," he said, "and at least let me look it over?"

I've learned never to ignore an eager buyer, so I retrieved the carton, dusted it off, and trundled it in the next morning.

"How much do want?" the dealer asked after rummaging through it.

"Seven hundred and fifty dollars," I said, figuring he'd pass on it, which was okay because I didn't mind keeping it.

"Done!" he said to my surprise, and in that instant I realized I'd asked too little.   I wondered how much he would have paid—$1,000 or $1,250?   My disappointment lasted only a moment. After all, I'd made a profit of $650 on something I'd owned for about seven years, which amounts to a gain of about 100 percent per year. Not bad for a $100 investment.

An east coast dealer tells the story of a blue collar worker who, back in the 1930s, began accumulating Japanese stamps. In those days, Japan—busy with its military adventures in China—was held in much the same esteem as Nazi Germany. Americans didn't want Japanese stamps and dealers were happy to unload them. During the war, he was able to buy them even more cheaply. He bought and bought, all through the years. By the 1970s, he had an accumulation worth more than a million dollars! All on a modest income.

So, keep your eyes open for material that seems out of vogue, but for which a future potential market exists. Being a contrarian can pay off.

General Comments. Unused stamps generally appreciate at a faster rate than used stamps, except in the case of some rarities.

Pay attention to esthetics. Eye appeal is important.

A large market exists for moderately priced stamps. Over the years, mass marketers have done extensive market research into the buying habits of the public. They discovered that $29 is about the threshold of impulse buying. Buyers don't give too much thought to purchases of less than $29. Above $29, they consider more carefully, and the higher the price the more carefully they consider. There would seem to be plenty of room for price appreciation in scarce, but moderately priced stamps.

Stamps with topical appeal offer more potential for appreciation than their counterparts without topical appeal. For example, in 1994 the United States issued a set of stamps in conjunction with the World Cup, which is the world championship of soccer. Soccer is the most widely played and popular sport in the world, everywhere, it seems, but America.   The   World   Cup commemorative stamps were ignored by American collectors, but are now (at this writing in 1997) in great demand among foreign topical collectors, so much so that the stamp is worth a premium above face value just three years after its release. Not a big premium, but more of a premium than other stamps issued in 1994. I'm not suggesting that the World Cup stamps would have been a worthwhile speculation as a new issue. I'm just pointing out that other things being equal, a topically popular stamp stands a better chance for appreciation.

Arbitrage

Arbitrage opportunities arise from differences in stamp markets from country to country and from differences in the value of currencies. Arbitrage opportunities also arise because of the insularity of individual foreign national stamp markets. Arbitrage opportunities are usually first recognized by dealers and collectors specializing in those countries.

An arbitrage opportunity often exists when large, competitive buy ads began to appear in philatelic weeklies. When a number of dealers begin offering to buy, say, China, Japan, and Far East, it's usually a sign that prices abroad are higher than reflected in stamp catalogues.

The stamp market is global. Pricing differences exist because the market for each nation's stamps is established in that nation. Most nations with large established collector bases publish annual specialized stamp catalogues with prices for their nation's stamps—*Gibbons* in Great Britain, *Michel* for Germany, *Yvert* for France, and so on. Each nation's specialized catalogue tends to be more in tune with what's going on in its own market than are generalized catalogues published abroad. That's due in part to the fact that there are simply too many stamps and too much information for general catalogues to stay on top of.

Spot arbitrage opportunities by comparing prices in foreign specialized catalogues with prices in U.S. catalogues. You'd be surprised at how many prices in foreign catalogues are either higher or lower than prices listed in U.S. catalogues. And the differences are often overlooked by the average collector, and even many dealers.

Catalogue arbitrage opportunities arise from discrepancies in prices between catalogues. I recall buying never-hinged German Posthorn sets for $600 (60 percent of the then $1,000 U.S. catalogue value) aware that the price for never-hinged sets in the *Michel Katalog*, published in Germany, was $3,000 per set. I sold the sets to German dealers for $1,200 a set, which was more than full U.S. catalogue price. I sold wholesale and still doubled my money. That's how catalogue arbitrage works.

Sometimes prices listed in foreign catalogues are two, three, even four times or more than prices listed in domestic catalogues. Opportunities also arise because markets are fluid from country to country and since catalogues are usually published only once a year, market prices may be out of synch with catalogue prices. For example, a few years ago, the 1949 Italian Universal Postal Union stamp listed for $7.50 in U.S. catalogues, while at the same time selling for $85 in Italy. So compare prices in U.S. catalogues, foreign catalogues, and published buy prices. Sharp traders subscribe to foreign stamp periodicals to stay abreast of foreign buy prices, which are sometimes higher than domestic catalogue prices. The firm STAMPFINDERS published a series of books on price performance some of which include tabular listings of price discrepancies between U.S. and foreign specialized catalogues. *Refer to the* Resource Guide.

Foreign catalogues also list varieties (often with huge prices) that U.S. catalogues ignore. Sometimes you can pick these up for the price of the more common variety and profit handsomely.

Take time to learn the nuances of foreign markets. The nuances often affect value in ways that might not immediately be apparent to Americans. For example, Germans are very fussy about wanting their stamps to have uniform perforations. Americans, on the other hand, pay more attention to gum and hinging.

Currency arbitrage occurs when the difference in values of two currencies creates an opportunity for profit. When the dollar is weak or weakening, foreign dealers actively buy stamps in the United States, and when it's increasing in value, American dealers use the advantage to buy abroad.

A hypothetical example. If the Japanese yen rises from 120 per dollar to 100 yen per dollar, it means that each dollar a Japanese dealer spends in this country costs only 100 yen instead of 120 yen. It's the same as a sixteen-percent discount. He can afford to pay $10 (1,000 yen) for a stamp that would have cost him 1,200 yen before the value of the yen increased.

Sometimes arbitrage opportunities combine both catalogue and currency arbitrage.

NEW ISSUES

During the decades between 1930 and 1980, conventional wisdom held that mint sheets and plate blocks of commemorative new issues were a foolproof investment. It was a seductive notion, buying something inexpensive at cost (face value) without transaction fees and without need for special knowledge or sophistication. Something you could put away and send the kids to college on.

Following World War II, affluent collectors salted away millions of commemorative new issues creating an enormous overhang of supply, which remained invisible because buyers held on for that "someday" when they would be worth "a lot."

No one realized just how many millions of stamps had been salted away. I certainly didn't. Even after I got into the stamp business full-time, I reasoned that sooner or later they had to dry up, so I tucked them away as they came in—collection after collection. Soon my stock was bulging with mint sheets and plate blocks. I wanted to be prepared for the day when supplies dried up. But supplies didn't dry up. The hoards kept coming.

They didn't contain the key stamps, such as the $5 Liberty definitive, which dealers were paying $40 or more for. *If only they had bought $5 Liberties instead of sheets and sheets of commemoratives,* I thought, *I'd have stamps I could really use and they'd have made a profit on their investment.* But that's not the way it worked. The hoarding mentality seemed to prefer quantity over quality. After all, why spend $5 on a single stamp when you can get three commemorative sheets of 50 three-cent stamps for $4.50 and have half a buck left over.

Finally after three decades, I began to realize that common commemoratives weren't going to dry up. Perhaps it was the hoard of mint sheets I bought from Montana or the trunks full of plate blocks that began to change my mind. The Montana hoard contained more than $15,000 worth of three- and four-cent sheets—thousands of sheets of stamps, piles several feet tall! The trunk hoard contained bricks of three-cent plate blocks—1,000 plate blocks to the brick! The straw that finally broke the camel's back was the fellow who offered to sell me $234,000 worth of mint sheets in the mid-1980s. He had saved a pad (100 sheets of stamps) of every new issue. I passed on it. About that time I decided to thin my stock. No use tying up thousands of dollars in inventory when it's coming through the door faster than you can sell it. About the same time, I stopped buying new issues from the Postal Service. So did a lot of other dealers. We had grown accustomed to replenishing our inventory from the hoards of new issues that came through the door as discount postage.

Over the years, the cost of postage increased, as did the number of new issues. Hoarding new issues got more and more expensive. By the early 1980s, collectors began to realize that their accumulations of new issues were little more than discount postage, worth only 70 to 80 percent of face value. They stopped buying multiples and bought only the minimum number necessary for their collections.

By the late 1980s, dealers began to notice a paucity of duplicates in collections. Recently issued stamps began to appear on buy lists at or above face value. The broad, fundamental shift away from hoarding new issues had begun to make itself felt in the secondary market. The overhanging supply, the vast reservoir of hoarded duplicates that dealers had become so accustomed to tapping, disappeared. And because dealers had stopped buying new issues, they had little stock.

Ironically, the expense of collecting the mind-numbing number of new issues now seems to assure that collectors will keep only the minimum necessary and that these new issues will be worth more than their much-hoarded counterparts of decades gone by.

And, ironically, now that hoarding new issues has fallen out of favor, the strategy of buying them appears to make more sense than when they were all the rage. However, the return from buying and holding new issues must be weighed against the return from alternative use of the money.

The premium commanded by recent new issues, while heartening, is hardly cause to begin stockpiling them. Remember that new issues should gain at least as much annually as the most conservative interest rate in order to justify holding them as an investment. Each dollar's worth of new issues purchased in 1988 would have to be worth at least $1.62 in 1998 in order to match the same yield in savings at a conservative five-percent return.

At the moment, dealers are paying only face value to perhaps face plus 10 to 20 percent for selected recent new issues. There are a few exceptions, but not many. Not enough to justify returning to the old strategy of hoarding them.

Buying new issues *en masse* in the hope of getting the occasional winner makes about as much sense as buying every new penny stock in order to make sure you get the next IBM or Microsoft. When you buy broadly, the non-performers more than offset gains realized from the few that perform.

Remember, not everything ignored by buyers will gain favor in the future. The trick is to figure out which will and take a position. That makes for an interesting speculation.

The problem with a book or periodical recommending specific items is that the opportunities are largely rendered invalid when a mass of readers all jump on it. It makes more sense to try to recognize opportunities on your own and keep quiet about them.

The following example illustrates what happens when the mass of buyers does the same thing at the same time.

As mentioned earlier, collectors should have saved the $5 Liberty definitive stamp instead of three-cent commemoratives. In the late 1970s, hoarders noticed the sharp rise in price of the $5 Liberty definitive and its predecessor the $5 Presidential, both of which sold for several hundred dollars at the time. They started buying then-current $5 J.B. Moore definitive plate blocks, no doubt reasoning that they were destined to perform in the same way.

The Postal Service was happy to oblige them. One philatelic clerk boasted of selling $5 J.B. Moore plate blocks to "investors" a hundred at a time. It didn't take me long to realize that $5 J.B. Moore plate blocks offered little potential for appreciation. Because collectors bought vast numbers of $5 J.B. Moore plate blocks, they still trade as discount postage.

Buyers should have been looking for what no one else was buying—not what had gone up in the past. And as soon as everyone hopped on the $5 J.B. Moore bandwagon, smart money should have hopped off. Once an opportunity becomes common knowledge, the target is overbought, which stifles subsequent appreciation.

Be careful not to engage in faulty reasoning. Try to determine what current buyers are ignoring, which will be in demand later. And remember, not everything that collectors are ignoring will necessarily be in demand later.

For example, one collector bragged that he was accumulating addressed, uncacheted new first-day covers because everyone else was buying cacheted, unaddressed first-day covers. He would have the only ones, he reasoned, and could charge whatever he wanted for them. He didn't take into account that the reason no one else sent away for new, addressed, uncacheted first-day covers was because they found them unattractive.

In the early years, collectors collected addressed, uncacheted first day covers because that's the way they came. As the market grew more sophisticated, collectors insisted on cacheted covers without addresses because they didn't want someone else's name cluttering their covers. Besides, cacheted covers were more visually appealing and addresses detracted from a cover's esthetics. So, addressed, uncacheted first-day covers fell out of favor and are not likely to again return to favor. There is little likelihood that our would-be speculator will find much of a market for his covers regardless of how rare they are.

Another fellow bought up United Nations stamps because they could be had for half face value. He reasoned that when demand later increased, he could sell them for a handsome profit. It was an interesting speculation.

Virtually the entire press run of each new United Nations issue ends up in the hands of collectors. Almost none are used on mail. And collectors hoarded them extensively during the 1950s through 1970s. They can be used for postage, but only at U.N. headquarters in New York. That's why they sell for such a great discount from face value. If they weren't valid for postage in New York, they would sell for even less.

Our speculator bought and bought and bought. Thousands and thousands of dollars worth of mint U.N. postage. I questioned his reasoning because all during the 1960s and 1970s I had seen vast numbers of U.N. stamps come through the door, but rarely had a customer ask for any. Everyone who collected U.N. stamps seemed to have them, precisely because they were so cheap. I tried to point out to him that he would run out of money long before the supply of mint U.N. stamps was exhausted. But he would have none of it. He kept buying and buying. This went on for several years, until, at last, he realized that the reason U.N. stamps were so cheap was because there was no demand for them and because the supply was unlimited. Finally, he decided to dump them, and even then had trouble finding anyone interested in tying up thousands of dollars in dead inventory.

Heavily promoted foreign new issues with transitory themes such as World Refugee Year, the Royal Wedding, and even the American Bicentennial rarely increase in value enough to offset their original cost. They are referred to as "omnibus" issues when nations all over the world issue stamps to mark a common theme. Completing collections of omnibus issues usually costs hundreds or thousands of dollars. There is little demand for them once the excitement of the event commemorated has passed, so dealers are reluctant to buy them.

Pay attention to what will be in demand. Remember, all new issues—including foreign new issues—are speculative. Few offer any opportunity for profit. The exceptions are covered in the next chapter.

SPECULATION

A speculator is defined as one who takes part in a risky venture with the hope of making a large, quick profit.

Speculative opportunities arise from time to time in new issues. Speculation can be triggered by a perceived shortage of stamps, a less than normal on-sale time, or even a feeling that the issue is too expensive and will not be saved in sufficient numbers to meet future demand. It can be a mass phenomenon or isolated to a relatively few players.

Whatever the case, the strategy should be to anticipate demand, get in, ride the wave, then get out. Once the initial enthusiasm has runs its course, the object of speculation rarely makes significant additional gains.

In 1976, the Postal Service released a commemorative sheet of fifty stamps containing one each of the fifty state flags. It was the first time the Postal Service had ever issued a sheet containing fifty different designs and it was an immediate hit.

A normal sheet of commemoratives contained fifty copies of the same stamp. Speculators reasoned that the state-flags sheet would be fifty times scarcer than a normal commemorative and the rush was on. The stamp market was hot at the time, flush with money, which helped fuel the speculative frenzy.

I, too, felt the state-flags sheet would be a good play. I bought ten pads (a pad contains 100 sheets) at face value ($650 per pad) shortly before it went off sale and waited. I had $6,500 invested.

Before long, dealer buy ads began appearing. They edged up week by week. When the price reached $8.50 per sheet, I sold eight of the ten pads for $6,800, recovering my original investment. I had two pads left to ride out the speculation.

The price continued to rise: $9 . . . $9.50 . . . $10 . . . $10.50.

I knew that the item wasn't really scarce. Everyone seemed to have plenty. It just appeared to be scarce. In any case, the buy price continued to climb because speculators were holding out in anticipation of even higher prices. Sooner or later, someone holding a large quantity would unload and the buy offers would disappear overnight. The only question was, how high would the price go before it happened.

At $11 per sheet, I started to get nervous. At $12 per sheet, I decided "A profit in hand is worth two in blue sky." So I bailed out, reaping a profit of $2,400 in the space of a couple of months. The price of the state-flags sheet continued to rise. Eventually it reached $20 per sheet. Perhaps I should have felt stupid for bailing out so early. But I didn't. I've never regretted taking a profit. My philosophy is, take a profit and move on to the next item rather than hold out for the last buck.

Eventually, the bubble burst and the price plummeted. And now, more than 20 years later, the buy price for state-flags sheets hovers around $7.50.

In November 1989, the Postal Service issued a set of three souvenir sheets in conjunction with World Stamp Expo held in Washington, DC. I asked the postal clerks at the show how the sheets were selling and learned that most collectors were buying only one or two sets. Armed with that knowledge and a hunch, I decided to buy a few hundred sets. Twenty-four months later, I sold them to another dealer for double what I had paid for them. Unlike the state-flags speculation, few participated in the World Stamp Expo speculation, and prices for the sheets has not softened.

In the first example, the price rose because a large number of players squeezed supply in anticipation of rising prices. In the second example, the price rose because collectors ignored the issue and supplies were genuinely thin. In both cases, the speculation paid off.

The recalled Legends of the West sheet, too, is a classic example of how new-issue speculations behave. The compact sheet of twenty old-West subjects included a portrait of Bill Pickett, an early black rodeo star. After the sheets were printed and distributed to post offices, but before they were put on sale, a member of Pickett's family objected that the portrait appearing on the stamp was not Bill Pickett's.

The Postal Service ordered the stamps recalled from post offices and announced that it would print a revised sheet with the correct portrait. In the meantime, some sheets had been inadvertently sold early—one buyer even announcing that his purchase would be worth a million dollars—and many collectors felt that the Postal Service should issue the stamps, or at least make some available to collectors. The decision to recall the issue created a firestorm of controversy.

The Postal Service finally announced that it would make 150,000 sheets available to collectors by a lottery system, one sheet per customer. The announcement set off a speculative frenzy. Everyone knew the sheets would be worth more than their cost of $6.75, but how much was the question. Rumors abounded. Many, if not most, sent in multiple entries, often in the name of relatives, pets, even imaginary persons. Part of it was greed, part of it a genuine concern that only one of every three or four entries would be filled. Dealers, collectors, and stamp writers compared prices for earlier stamps of similar quantity—such as the White Plains souvenir sheet of 1926, which at the time sold in the $400 to $600 range—to get a feel for where the price might settle out. The best guesses predicted a price of $200 to $400.

Having been in the stamp business for many years, I knew that customers for modern $400 items were few and far between. Most collectors follow the path of least resistance. They buy recent issues—which are the most economical—and work their way backwards. They tend to prefer less expensive stamps and postpone buying more expensive stamps. Based on my experience, I didn't think the market would support a $400 modern issue. I questioned whether it would support a $200 issue. I felt that a lot of collectors would eventually rationalize not buying the sheet.

In the meantime, I sent in my order, as did my wife, and we waited. I received one of the sheets soon after the Postal Service began awarding them. I called several dealer friends to get a handle on the market, but no one seemed to have a firm idea of where the market should be. Collectors were bombarding us with calls wanting to know how much the sheets were worth. Calls from potential sellers greatly outnumbered those from potential buyers. Owners of sheets were phoning daily to check on the state of the market. In the meantime, dealers struggled to figure out what fair buying and selling prices ought to be. The consensus seemed to be that you couldn't go wrong paying $100 per sheet. On the retail side, prices ranged from $125 to $200. The point of price resistance seemed to be $200. Collectors just didn't want to pay more than that. At the same time, potential sellers were holding out for bigger bucks, the rumored $200 to $400. Dealers moved the sheets as fast as they came in because they didn't want to be caught holding the bag.

I realized that the market would not reach $400; $200 seemed more realistic. Those who telephoned daily to check prices, who were holding out for the last buck, seemed to think that it was only a matter of time before the sheet reached $400 and that $600 was likely. They became irate when offered $150. The recalled Legends of the West sheet never came even remotely close to the $400 level. The market softened relatively quickly, and now several years later, the sheet remains modestly priced with a buy/sell spread in the $125/$150 range.

Collectors constantly speculate on new issues, most of which never take off. A few years ago, the Postal Service began selling limited quantities of some stamps in uncut press sheets, which could be separated into gutter pairs and other interesting configurations. Some felt that because of the limited quantities, these stamps offered potential for increase in value. And based on the numbers released, the reasoning seemed sound. The only problem is that no real collector demand for uncut press sheets has developed. And collector demand is what causes prices to rise over the long term. Aside from a couple of issues, such as the Bugs Bunny imperforate variety released in a small quantity, which initially soared in price but quickly fell back to a more modest and stable price level, there has not been much demand for or price appreciation in uncut press sheets. Those who got in early on Bugs Bunny and got out at the peak made money; those who bought later at the higher price level, did not—and are not likely to.

If uncut press sheets and their various configurations ever catch on, those who speculated on them may make out. If press sheets don't catch on, they will have gambled and lost. My guess is that press sheets will not catch on because they cannot be conveniently mounted in albums and because they are expensive. Collectors have trouble just keeping up with the regular new issues, and few seem inclined to branch off into something so esoteric—and costly.

A speculative situation arises from unexpected demand (often brought about by the activity of speculative hoarding itself) or a shortage of supply, either real or perceived. Either way, the speculation lasts as long as there are more buyers than sellers. Once an item becomes the object of speculation, sellers hold in anticipation of further price increases and continue to hold so long as price continues to rise. No one wants to sell until the last nickel can be extracted. Speculative markets operate on waves of optimism and pessimism. And in their euphoria, speculators tend to imagine unrealistically high peaks. All speculative markets outrun their potential, and often, relatively quickly.

So, get in, ride the wave, and get out.

STATISTICAL TOOLS

Information is the key to every intelligent decision. The more information you have, the better your investment decisions will be. Gather information to achieve the broadest view of the market possible. An array of information is more useful than any individual bit.

Printing Statistics. Printing statistics give a basic idea of relative scarcity. However, they must be weighed against demand because demand not supply drives price.

I once had a customer who planned his stamp investment purchases according to quantity printed. He studied printing statistics religiously and quoted them at every opportunity. He believed that there existed a predictable ratio between price and quantity—that quantity determined price. He further reasoned that at some point the market would recognize this relationship and prices for underpriced (according to printing statistics) stamps would rise to find their "natural" level.

He scoured dealers for his favorites—imperforates of the Alaska-Yukon issue of 1909, the Hudson-Fulton issue of 1909, and the Harding memorial issue of 1923. He cleaned them out and they gladly obliged, for there was little demand for the stamps.

For my own part, I doubted that collectors would abandon their traditional habits and start buying stamps according to printing statistics. I tried to explain to him that his logic was flawed, that the stamps were expensive, and that collectors tended to postpone buying expensive stamps so long as they had spaces for inexpensive stamps to fill. But he would have none of it. So, in the end, I kept quiet and sold him the stamps he wanted. This went on for several years. He accumulated thousands of dollars worth, sure that prices would soon rise. But prices for his stamps never rose more quickly than for other stamps. Eventually he quit buying. The market outlasted him. To this day, I'm still not sure that he understands that the market does not value stamps according to printing statistics. It values them according to demand.

Quantity Surviving. The number of stamps surviving and available to the market is more important than the number printed. Some stamps, such as the Zeppelin airmails of 1930, were purchased almost exclusively by collectors. Most of the issued quantity survives in philatelic hands. Others, such as definitives of the nineteenth century, were used on mail and few survive.

The number surviving can never be known with certainty, but one indicator is the frequency with which a stamp appears at auction. Although not originally intended as an investment tool, *The Buyer's Guide* provides some insight into relative scarcity of key issues. The book lists the average frequency that a stamp appears at auction based on a survey of about 100,000 auction realizations. The frequency with which a stamp appears at auction gives a pretty good indication of its relative scarcity.

Price Indexes. The most common type of price index is based on retail prices of a basket of selected issues. Stamp price indexes are supposed to mirror the state of the market in the same way that the Dow Jones Average reflects what's going on in the stock market.

Several have appeared over the years, including one I pioneered in the early 1970s in the *Datz Philatelic Index*. A revised version appeared in the *Scott StampMarket Update* in the early 1980s. Today, *Linn's Stamp News* publishes an index, which is revised monthly. Interestingly, all three indexes reveal that before the Great Boom, the trend line of prices remained fairly horizontal.

The line climbed steeply during the boom and descended nearly as steeply after the boom. After the correction, which took several years, the line straightened into a nearly horizontal line with only a slight incline, as illustrated in Figure 3. And if one were to factor in inflation—which has remained low since the boom—it would probably more than account for the gentle upward slope.

Stamp price indexes are useful for getting a general feel for how the market is behaving.

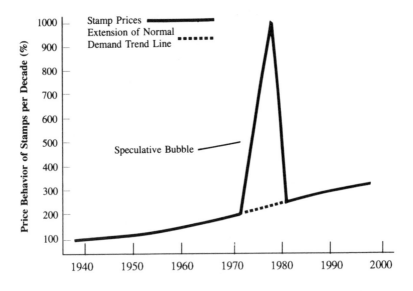

Figure 3. Stamp prices over the decades.

Index of Buying Activity.   One of the most useful tools, because it is a leading indicator, is a chart of buying activity. At this writing, no one publishes this information in graph form. In the early 1980s, the *Scott StampMarket Update* tracked wanted-to-buy ads appearing in philatelic weeklies (factoring in both the number of ads and the total column inches, adjusted to discount anomalous distortions, such as one-time full page ads) and published the results in graph form.

As a dealer, I realized years ago that when dealers find themselves short of stamps, they advertise to buy. When wanted-to-buy ads increase in both size and number, it means that the demand is growing stronger. When dealer buying activity increases, retail price increases are not far behind, and, ultimately, increases in catalogue prices. At this writing, only *Linn's Stamp News* publishes a survey of buying activity. It measures the percentage of buy ads to the aggregate of all adds, both buying or selling.

Salomon Brothers Report. During the late 1970s, Salomon Brothers, the New York investment banking firm, began issuing a series of annual reports comparing the performance of various financial and tangible assets. Stamps were included for the first time in the 1978 report, and much to the amazement of everyone ranked third (behind gold and Chinese ceramics) as the best performing asset during the period 1968-1979. Stamps showed a compounded annual return of 18.9 percent. Even more astonishing was the return listed for the previous one-year period, 60.9 percent! The report listed fourteen assets: gold, Chinese ceramics, stamps, rare books, silver, coins, old masters paintings, diamonds, oil, farmland housing, foreign exchange, bonds and stocks. According to the report, the consumer price index (CPI) for the period 1968-1979 posted an annual increase of 6.5 percent, and for the previous one-year period 10.5 percent. The CPI figures represent inflation (loss of purchasing power). By comparison, stocks increased only 5.3 percent during the previous year and averaged only 3.1 percent compounded annually during the previous ten-year period.

That and subsequent annual reports received much attention, both within the hobby and outside it. Within the hobby because it was viewed as evidence that the financial world had finally acknowledged stamps as "legitimate" investments. What the hobby overlooked or failed to realize was that the report was intended to promote the idea that financial investments were undervalued—not promote tangibles. The initial report was entitled "Stocks Are the Only Bargains Left." The text of that report contained a well-researched analysis of the points Salomon Brothers thought indicated an opportunity for investors in stocks. The report mentioned tangibles only in passing. The message seemed clear—smart money buys when equities are undervalued in anticipation of a run-up, not at its peak. Regardless of the report's intent, it was widely heralded within the hobby as recognition by Wall Street that stamps had arrived in the big leagues.

Had Wall Street really believed in the merits of stamps (or Chinese ceramics or coins) as investments, we would have seen a profusion of investment "products" packaged and marketed by brokerage firms. Wall Street was interested in promoting its historical products, not breaking new ground.

Bear in mind, that statistical increases in financial assets largely pass to the investor intact. Statistical increases in collectibles do not readily reflect net gains to investors because sizable markups must be subtracted.

Auction Prices Realized. Auction prices realized are an excellent tool for market price information, but sadly no firm has been able to make a go of publishing such information, although several have tried. The truth is, most collectors aren't interested in up-to-the-minute market information because they are more attuned to what they want than to how much they will have to pay for it. Besides, they are used to referring to catalogues for price information and often appear to find auction prices realized arrays confusing and intimidating.

Tracking Values. Stamps can't be tracked on a ticker tape. They are usually monitored on a slower basis, like the passing of seasons rather than daily weather.

Stamps don't increase at a predictable or steady rate. Sometimes they go for several years without much movement, then experience a spurt in a relatively short period of time. When averaged out, the gain may translate into an excellent annual return. Most experienced investors follow the maxim, "Buy right and the stamps will take care of themselves."

Catalogues list yearly changes in value. In the interim, advertised retail prices, buying prices, and auction prices give the best indication of changing values.

Fundamental analysis is more useful when making slow-moving, longer term investments, which stamp often turn out to be.

Technical analysis is more useful for short term investing. Sometimes we are confronted by too much statistical data and tend to be awed by it. Informal data, such as signs of an emerging trend, are often just as useful as statistical information, if not more so. Approach statistical information as just another piece of the puzzle and factor it into your overall view of the market.

WALL STREET

Those who believe in the merits of stamp investment have long dreamed of stamps catching the eye of Wall Street. The ideal vehicle for stamp investors would be a publicly traded fund managed by an experienced professional, which by virtue of its size could be administered inexpensively. But do stamps make sense for Wall Street?

During the late 1970s, I thought stamps were the ideal tangible asset for reasons enumerated earlier. The nation seemed poised on the brink of hyperinflation, economic collapse, even depression. No one seemed to know what was going to happen next. Everyone was worried. Tangibles seminars were all the rage. Speakers warned of all manner of catastrophes from global economic meltdown to government confiscation of wealth and panic in the streets. They hawked every sort of patent-medicine remedy from Swiss bank accounts and tax shelters to bags of survival silver, dehydrated food, home arsenals, and secluded acreages in Idaho and Montana upon which bunkers could be built.

While in Los Angeles to attend an economic seminar in 1980, I spent an afternoon with a retired investment banker at the suggestion of a mutual friend. He'd been a senior vice president of one of the best known brokerage firms in America. He was rumored to have been J. Paul Getty's personal stock broker. I'll call him Mr. Smith. We met at his home, which was vintage Beverly Hills: long cobblestone driveway, six-car garage, immaculate sprawling grounds dotted with palm trees.

I made my way up the drive and parked next to a suds-covered Rolls Royce that a young fellow was rinsing off with a garden hose. He directed me to the front door. I rang the bell. A white-jacketed butler greeted me and showed me through the house to the patio, a spacious expanse of pale-colored stone overlooking a California-sized, sea-green pool.

Mr. Smith was on the phone. He acknowledged me with a smile and motioned me to sit down. I felt overdressed in my pin-striped three-piece suit. Smith wore Bermuda shorts and a Hawaiian shirt. I sat and waited. The yard sloped away toward round, perfectly manicured shrubs, which were spaced between tall poplars that stood like pillars under the clear June sky.

Newspapers and magazines littered the glass-covered wrought-iron patio table between us. The financial pages of the *Wall Street Journal* lay in Smith's lap, marked with bold circles and notes.

Smith had invited me to his home to discuss the possibility of taking stamp investment to Wall Street. *This is the big time,* I thought as I waited for him to finish his phone call. Because of the voracious interest in tangibles, some Wall Street firms had begun exploring the feasibility of offering them to investors. I was as excited and apprehensive as someone on his first job interview.

"Bob says you're an expert on stamps," Smith said, hanging up the phone. Bob was our mutual acquaintance. "That you've written a book on stamp performance."

"Yes," I replied.

"I hope you don't mind, but I've invited a colleague, Jerry Jones, to sit in. He ought to be here any time. Jerry's senior VP of marketing, in charge of new products."

While we waited for Jones to appear, the white-gloved, white-jacketed butler served me a Coke in a tall, sterling-rimmed glass from a silver tray. I wanted to ask Smith about J. Paul Getty in the worst way, but I dared not. I let my eyes wander. The home had to be worth millions, I guessed. I'd never seen a more lovely yard.

"Do you collect?" I asked.

"No," he said. "Bob's been telling me a lot about stamps. They're little works of art. Fascinating. But, I've never had much time for hobbies." My eyes wandered, again, to the boldly annotated financial pages, and I understood where his passion lay.

Jones arrived in a light-gray suit, and I no longer felt overdressed. The butler offered him a soft drink and he settled into his chair. Smith got right down to business.

"Bob says stamps are *the* thing right now," he said.

"They've been appreciating rapidly," I acknowledged. "Up more than sixty percent last year." I pulled out a copy of my book, the *Datz Philatelic Index,* opened it to the appropriate page, and handed it to Smith to illustrate the point.

"Very impressive," he said studying the page, flipping through the book. "And they've never gone down in value?"

"That's right," I said. Smith appeared to be impressed. He handed Jones the book. Jones scanned it.

"Gold, real estate, diamonds, art, stamps—can you believe the growth," he asked, looking at Jones. "People act like the stock market's got the plague." I could tell by his tone that he couldn't understand why investors had deserted the stock market. Jones shrugged.

"How would we sell stamps?" Smith asked.

"Like a mutual fund," I said. "Professionals would put together and manage portfolios. Make buy and sell decisions, supervise the portfolios' growth."

"You could do something like that?"

"Yes," I said

"How much would it take to put a fund together?"

"A few million dollars," I said.

"It would have to be at least ten or twenty million, don't you think?" Smith said, turning toward Jones.

"Really wouldn't be worth bothering with under twenty," Jones agreed.

I couldn't believe my ears—ten or twenty *million* dollars. I tried to imagine the effect that kind of purchasing power would have on the stamp market.

"Could you spend fifty million . . . or a hundred million?" Smith asked. His eyes were pleasant, yet serious. "Are there that many stamps?"

I paused. "I suppose so," I said, struggling to imagine how one would spend fifty million dollars on stamps. The major auctions boasted grosses of five million dollars a year at the time. A hundred million dollars would suck the market dry.

"How about liquidity?" Smith asked.

"We'd sell in an orderly fashion," I said. "Utilize auctions and individual dealers. Naturally, you couldn't liquidate the portfolio all at once."

"How much could the market absorb at once?" Smith asked.

I'd never thought about it. It couldn't absorb a hundred million dollars worth of stamps in one shot, not even fifty million. I tried to imagine the impact of twenty million. Before I had a chance to answer, he asked, "How long would it take to get out?"

"I'm not sure," I said. I'd never thought about dumping a portfolio. I assumed the fund would be ongoing as long as it made money, which it should do if managed properly.

Jones looked skeptical, but said nothing. He took a sip from his silver-rimmed tumbler.

"Mmm," Smith said, nodding, deep in thought.

"How would you track increases in value?" Jones asked. Then, answering his own question, "You'd have to get appraisals."

"We'd know from market prices, " I said. "We'd calculate that from time to time."

"We'd have to get an independent opinion," Smith said. "To be prudent. For our own protection. Especially on something like this."

I nodded. "Well, appraisals wouldn't be a problem. It would add expense," I said, then as an afterthought, "but not that much, I suppose. It wouldn't be a problem."

The numbers raced through my mind. They seemed to be contemplating a project much larger than I had envisioned, and I grappled with the magnitude of it.

"What do you think, Jerry?" Smith said.

"I don't know if it makes sense for us," he said, sitting up in his chair, setting his drink on the glass table.

His reply startled me. I felt sure they wanted to get into the stamp investment business.

"First, we'd have to train our staff to sell the product. They don't know anything about stamps. Investors are going to have questions. Brokers have to have answers. That's going to take some time and expense."

I hadn't thought about that.

"And the size. Ten or twenty million's hardly worth bothering with. Especially considering we can blow out a hundred million dollar utility offering before noon without having to re-educate staff and with no risk."

Smith nodded.

"We'd have costs in promotional materials. And there's the question of registration. Which states we could sell in."

Jones outlined his views quickly and succinctly. Smith listened.

"The potential profit doesn't seem to justify the trouble and expense. I question whether it's a good fit for us."

I was crestfallen. Smith remained silent for a long moment, absorbed in thought.

"You've got a point," he said at length, glancing at Jones. "The project is too small. Wouldn't merit training the sales force." He took a sip from his glass. "The sales force is definitely a weak link. And liquidity." He set down the glass.

"Much as stamps sound interesting, I have to agree with Jerry," he said, turning toward me.

I knew as I left that day, that a publicly traded stamp fund was not likely to materialize. I knew that other brokerage firms would come to the same conclusion. Stamps would never make sense to Wall Street. I had to agree with them. How could the stamp market absorb ten or twenty million dollars worth of stamps at one time without distorting values? It couldn't.

Within a couple of years the tangibles craze was over, financial markets were booming, and the last thing Wall Street had on its mind was a rare stamp fund.

During the boom, I met with numerous brokers, pension plan administrators, and financial planners who were interested in stamps as investments. I discovered that all had one thing in common—they either collected stamps or had an interest in stamps, often from childhood. I never once met any financial professional even remotely interested in stamps as investments, who did not already have some knowledge or interest in stamps.

In the mid-1980s, the International Stamp Exchange tried to establish a centralized public marketplace. They rented upscale office space, printed a slick, full-color brochure that hyped the stamp market, quoting the grossly inflated figure of 20 million stamp collectors in the United States, and envisioned a central locus operated by "Members, Floor Brokers, and Member Brokers representing collectors and investors and daily buyers and sellers."

The exchange intended to list stamps on a private electronic network (each with a terminal and password—this was before the Internet) displaying the lowest bid price, the highest ask price, and the last trade. Members (individuals) could enter orders on their own account; brokers could trade stamps for clients from anywhere in the world; floor brokers would have offices in the exchange and be able to make trades on the floor, although a floor such as those in stock and commodity exchanges never really existed. It was a grandiose idea, but one doomed to failure for lack of interest.

Trades were to be accomplished through personal computers and telex connections, which would connect 2,500,000 personal computer users and enable them to receive quotations on rare stamps listed with the ISE. Stamps and payments would be sent to the exchange for verification and delivery. The idea was to allow stamps to be traded as easily as money can be deposited or withdrawn from a bank. One of the stated objectives of the ISE was to "permit the investment community to perceive rare stamps as an investment in the mainstream of financial products."

In addition, information compiled from trades would provide more timely price information than that available in catalogues. The problem of grading was addressed by creating a standardized grading system. For a standardized system to work, it must become "standard," which is to say accepted, used and even promoted by the collector and dealer establishment. If ever a field of individualists existed, it is in the stamp business. The standard grading system never got off the ground.

Had stamps lent themselves to sight-unseen trading and had collectors and dealers been inclined to change their traditional ways of doing business, the exchange might have had a chance. But, alas, the collecting community seems rooted in its ways. It's not that the philatelic community wanted the exchange to fail. They just ignored it and it faded away from lack of interest.

The financial community didn't pay much attention to it either. Most likely because stamps are not like financial products—and never will be. That is not to say that stamps cannot be good investments, but they must be approached for what they are—not for what it is unrealistic to expect them to be.

The promoter even blamed stamp-dealer self-interest for causing the exchange to fail, which is ridiculous. Nothing is more powerful than an idea whose time has come, and if it serves a need, the market will beat a path to its doorstep. The exchange failed because there was no demand for it. It was as if they gave a party and nobody came.

Conservation

Stamps are fragile objects that must be handled and stored with care. The three great enemies of stamps are light, heat and moisture. Avoid these hazards as much as possible.

Don't expose stamps to direct light for prolonged periods. Pigments are prone to fading, paper to yellowing. Sunlight is especially bad; fluorescent light not much better. Generally, stamps should not be framed and displayed in home or office. Even the use of UV glass to screen out ultraviolet light will not protect against other wavelengths, which too can cause damage over time, although more subtly. Short term exposure to light, such as exhibiting at a show, is not a danger.

More stamps are ruined by moisture than any other hazard. Moisture in all forms (water, humidity, dampness) is deadly. Keep stamps as dry as possible. Always store stamp albums upright so they can breathe. Never store albums flat, especially piled atop one another, because the weight causes stamps to stick, especially under humid conditions. Even stamps in glassines are susceptible to moisture and pressure. Once stuck together, only soaking will separate them, and their gum will be lost. Album paper absorbs humidity just like a sponge, but loses it only slowly. A few humid days can expose stamps to weeks of dampness. Whenever albums are exposed to abnormal humidity, open them afterwards and allow them to dry. If you live in a damp climate, consider airing stamps out several times a year to avoid gum glaze. Humidity wreaks such havoc on gum that some collectors in places such as Hawaii and the Caribbean islands, collect only used stamps.

Moisture also promotes the growth of mold and mildew, which discolors stamps and attacks gum. Even stamps without gum are susceptible to mildew and foxing.

Avoid storing stamps in places prone to dampness or leaks, such as basements, storage sheds, and barns. Don't store stamps near water pipes. Even safe deposit boxes are not one hundred percent safe. Stamps in fireproof bank vaults have been ruined by sprinklers set off by a fire in another part of the bank. Occasionally, safe deposit vaults located below ground level are flooded by broken water mains or springtime downpours, perils that do not affect vaults located above ground. Subterranean vaults are also more prone to dampness from ground water.

Keep stamps away from heat, which compounds the effects of moisture. Avoid storing stamp albums on shelves exposed to direct sunlight. Avoid attics and garages, which, likewise, are prone to overheating. Exposure to heat and moisture causes stamps to curl, often so badly that attempting to uncurl them ruins them. Dry heat is no better. It causes stamps to become brittle and gum to crack, which in severe cases breaks through a stamp's paper, ruining it. Prolonged exposure to dramatic temperature swings weakens a stamp's paper fibers over time, just as bending a piece of wire again and again weakens it.

Keep stamps away from dust and dirt. Windblown grit, the kind that accumulates in garages and sheds, acts like sandpaper, if ever so subtly. Keep stamps away from insects. Even seemingly innocuous ones can be dangerous. Crickets love the flavor of some gums and eagerly nibble away portions of stamps possessing it.

A few more don'ts. Never use any kind of tape to mount stamps or covers. Keep tape—adhesive, cellophane, whatever the kind—away from your stamps. Don't use it on stamps, on album pages, on glassines, or to secure the sides of mounts. Don't use tape on anything stamp-related—period.

Don't mount or store newspaper clippings next to stamps. Newspaper yellows and gets worse with the passing of time. The chemicals that cause yellowing migrate into any other papers they come in contact with—stamps, covers, album pages. Discard old glassines or anything else that has yellowed with age. The jury's still out on recycled paper, which is treated with powerful bleaching agents and other chemicals. In general, avoid papers with a strong chemical odor. It may take years to know what effects, if any, recycling chemicals have on paper. In the meantime, avoid taking risks with your stamps.

Keep rubber bands away from stamps. They contain a sulphur compound that discolors some pigments. And there's nothing worse than a rubber band that's dried out or melted, and adhered to whatever it was in contact with.

Don't use paper clips on stamps or anywhere that might leave a mark on stamps. Some paper clips rust, especially in humid climates, leaving spots on anything they've come in contact with.

Avoid storing stamps in anything made of softened plastic such as vinyl. The softer the plastic, the more softening agent (visible as an oily iridescent film). The softening agent, which is petro-chemical based, has been known to leech the color out of some printing inks and to discolor stamps. Unsoftened (free of softening agent) vinyl is fairly inert. Avoid putting two types of plastic in proximity because of potential chemical interaction. Don't interleave mounts with other plastic sheets. Make sure stamps are dry of watermark fluid before inserting into mounts.

Don't store stamps in variety-store photo albums, especially the kind with waxed or self-adhesive pages, even those advertised as being low-tack.

Always use a mount large enough to comfortably accommodate a stamp. Never force a stamp into a mount too small or too tightly fitting. You'll either damage the stamp right then, or it will warp if the mount shrinks with the passing of time. And be careful not too use too much saliva on the back of a mount. The excess will leak onto the back of the stamp, defeating the whole purpose of the mount.

Don't hinge never-hinged stamps. You'll reduce their value. It's okay to hinge used stamps and stamps with no gum.

Don't remove stamps from covers or postcards; they're usually worth more than the stamps by themselves. Don't attempt to separate stamps that are stuck together or stuck down to album pages; you'll only cause damage and reduce their value. Don't attempt to clean stamps; you'll do more harm than good.

A few do's.

Make sure your hands are clean before working with stamps and always use stamp tongs to handle stamps. Fingers contain moisture, oil, and often small amounts of grime.

Keep food and drink away from stamps. Remove stamps from holders carefully to avoid damage.

Use materials made specifically for the hobby to store stamps. If it wasn't made for stamps, think twice about using it. Several companies manufacture high-quality supplies for stamps. *Refer to the* Resource Guide.

Insure stamps if they have any significant value. Most homeowner's policies cover collectibles, but their limits of liability are low, typically $300 or so, without a special rider. The APS offers an excellent, low cost policy that covers most risks, fire, theft, etc. Their policy's limits of liability are higher and premiums lower than those of most standard casualty policies. *Refer to the* Resource Guide.

Insurance is often less expensive than paying safe deposit rent, especially for bulky collections. Before spending hundreds of dollars a year on storage, compare the cost with insurance. Be aware that unless the contents of a safe deposit box are insured, they're at risk from loss by fire, theft, natural disaster, etc. Virtually all banks refuse to accept liability for the contents of a safe deposit box for any reason. Check your box rental agreement.

When shipping stamps, pack them securely with the idea that if something can be damaged, it will be. Use registered mail for the best protection.

In summary, use common sense in handling and storing stamps. Keep them away from light, heat, moisture, and dirt. Avoid storing stamps in basements, garages, storage sheds, and attics. To the degree possible, store stamps in an area with reasonably constant temperature and humidity. Use high quality materials, those intended specifically for use with stamps, where possible. Insure stamps that have significant value.

FAKES & FORGERIES

Stamps have been faked almost since day one, both common stamps and rarities alike. Some fakes are ridiculously crude and easy to spot, others are clever and fool all but the most practiced eye. There's not room here to cover the subject in depth, however, you should be aware that fakes and forgeries exist and know how to protect yourself.

Overprints and cancels are among the easiest things to fake. The Kansas-Nebraska overprints of 1929 have been extensively faked, especially used copies, because the underlying stamps are cheap and readily available. Cancels are often faked to increase the value of stamps that are common in unused condition but rare in used condition. Several of the German inflation issues of the early 1920s fall into that category. Mint copies of the stamps are common because they were inflated to worthlessness overnight and few were used on mail.

Used stamps are sometimes bleached to remove cancels. One of the favorite targets of bleaching is the U.S. ten-cent stamp of 1847, which was printed in black. Black printers' ink is less susceptible to fading in bleach than other printing inks and the difference in price between a used copy and a mint copy is several thousand dollars. Early stamps with pen cancels are often bleached either to make them appear unused or so that a device cancel can be added. Device-cancelled stamps are worth more than pen-cancelled stamps. Bleaching can often be detected by dipping a stamp in watermark fluid or examining it under ultraviolet light.

Special cancellations or markings are often added to inexpensive covers to increase their value. Sometimes common stamps are removed from a cover and replaced with stamps that are more valuable when used on cover.

Expensive first-day covers are sometimes faked with bogus cancels. Often fakes can be caught with a second look and a watchful eye. For example, a rubber-stamp cancel on an early issue known only with machine cancels. Rubber-stamp ink is gray, machine-applied ink is solid black. Remember, the experienced eye is always skeptical.

Perforated stamps can be trimmed to simulate imperforate varieties, and perforations can be added to imperforate stamps to simulate perforated varieties. This type of fakery is most often encountered on early U.S. stamps where stamps of similar design exist both perforate and imperforate, but with different values.

Examine potential purchases carefully. Buy from established, reputable sources. Read up on fakes and forgeries. Insist on expert certificates for expensive stamps. *Refer to the* Resource Guide.

Regumming. Regumming is endemic on unused stamps of the nineteenth century and on many stamps of the early twentieth century. As a rule of thumb, the earlier the stamp, the more likely its original gum will be gone. So check carefully. Don't be fooled by the comment that a stamp could not be regummed because the seller got it out of an old album or collection. Regumming has been going on for years.

Regumming is done to improve the appearance of a stamp, usually one that has been heavily hinged or lost its original gum. It's also done to cover faults such as thins, ironed-out creases or closed tears. These kinds of faults can be detected by dipping a stamp in watermark fluid. If they're beneath the gum, the stamp's been regummed. Faults usually show up darker than the surrounding paper, except in the case of filled thins, which show up lighter and are slower to dry when removed from the fluid. Watermark fluid is actually used much more extensively to spot faults than for checking watermarks.

Regumming jobs vary from crude to almost undetectable. The majority are easy to spot. Original gum is applied before stamps are perforated. When stamps are torn apart, the paper fibers at the tips of the perforations "feather." Under magnification you can see tiny fibers sticking out. When stamps are regummed the liquid glue tends to soak into perforation tips, making them rigid and hard. Feel perforation tips to see if they are soft and pliable or rigid and hard. Pros often rub perforation teeth on the skin just above their lips, which is extremely sensitive. If the teeth feel rigid and hard, chances are the stamp's been regummed.

Regumming is usually applied with a brush. Look for brush marks or uneven application. Look for paper fibers or bubbles in the gum. You'd be surprised how sloppy some "stamp mechanics" are. One of the easiest and most useful methods of spotting regumming is to compare suspicious gum with the gum on genuine examples of the same set or series. Gum can be aged and colored to simulate original gum, but it's almost impossible to duplicate the appearance of the original—the exact texture, thickness, gloss, and evenness of application. So take time to familiarize yourself with what original gum looks like and compare suspect stamps to known genuine examples. Low values of sets make useful comparison specimens.

Remember that on the first few issues of U.S. stamps, gum was applied by hand with brushes from batches that often varied in color and consistency from one to the next and was often applied unevenly, sometimes leaving brush strokes. Original gum on some early stamps looks so bad that those unfamiliar with it often assume that it could not possibly be original. So take this into account. It is not possible to cover the subject in depth here, but it is thoroughly covered in the book *How to Detect Altered, Repaired and Damaged Stamps. Refer to the* Resource Guide.

An enthusiastic, yet naive collector once offered me a complete set of 1893 Columbians, the first U.S. commemoratives, in never-hinged condition. The words "never-hinged" immediately made me suspicious. I'd never seen or heard of a complete set in never-hinged condition. I removed the stamps from the plastic stocksheet and turned them over one by one.

"They're regummed," I said when I'd finished. "All except the one- and two-cent values."

The seller was aghast. "How do you know?" he insisted.

I had replaced the stamps face down on the stocksheet as I examined them.

"Look," I said. "No two gums are alike, except the two low values. Fifteen different types of gum on sixteen stamps. The Columbians are known to exist with three types of gum, but not fifteen."

Some stamps had thick gum, some had thin gum, some had yellow gum, some had white gum, some had gray gum. A couple even had tiny bubbles, fibers or brush marks on the gum. They might have been convincing when viewed one at a time, but together they had a patchwork appearance.

"Now for the clincher," I said. I turned out the lights and exposed the stamps to ultraviolet light. Each stamp fluoresced differently—grays, violets, yellows, whites.

"You should have gotten certificates when you bought them," I said.

I checked his banknote issues and Trans-Mississippis. They'd been regummed as well. When I'd finished, I told him his stamps were worth around five to six thousand dollars.

"I spent more than twenty thousand dollars!" he exclaimed.

I think he doubted my opinion. He picked up the stamps and left.

He returned a few months later. He'd submitted the stamps for certification. They'd all come back as regummed. I wasn't in the market for regummed stamps, so I advised him to auction them. I later learned that he had gotten a little over $5,500 for the entire group. He could have saved himself a lot of money and heartache if he had educated himself *before* buying.

You can spot regummed rotary press stamps by checking to see if they contain gum-breaker ridges, which were applied during manufacture to prevent finished sheets from curling. Look at almost any commemorative stamp issued during the 1940s or early 1950s to see what gum-breaker ridges look like. It's virtually impossible to simulate gum-breaker ridges when regumming.

Unused rotary press issues without gum breakers have been regummed.

Sometimes disturbed gum is liquified and carefully redistributed—often with an artist's watercolor brush—to improve its appearance. The result can resemble regumming, although technically it is not.

Remember, few nineteenth century stamps exist in never-hinged condition and that the earlier the stamp, the more likely it is to have been regummed. If you're spending more than a few dollars on a stamp, get it expertized.

Reperforating. Reperforating is performed to enhance the appearance and value of stamps. Straight-edged stamps are often reperforated. Imperforate stamps are sometimes reperforated to simulated perforated stamps, especially expensive coils. Occasionally, stamps are reperforated to improve centering.

Examine perforations under a magnifying glass. The edges of reperforated holes often appear cleaner than those of normally perforated stamps. The reperforator's tool is most often a razor-sharp metal punch that cuts holes cleanly, unlike the equipment used in mass production, which leaves holes less perfectly punched and often less perfectly round.

Sometimes the stamp will "gauge" right, but the reperforated holes will be either larger of smaller than the genuine holes. In other cases, the spacing of holes is not the same as on genuine stamps. Pros often lay a suspect stamp atop a genuine example to see if the size and spacing of holes matches.

Examine perforation tips. The tips of normal perforations are somewhat uneven from having been pulled apart during separation. If the tips look flat—as if they are an interrupted straight edge—it's a good bet the stamp's been reperforated. Reperforators sometimes scrape at perf tips with a sharp instrument in an attempt to feather the edges and make them appear more normal. This is almost always evident under magnification. Again, compare the look of the suspect tips under magnification with those on genuine stamps.

Opposite rows of perforations should be parallel. If they're not, chances are the stamp has been reperforated. Many reperforating jobs are done one hole at a time, which makes it difficult to keep them in a straight line. So check to make sure that holes are in a straight line. After a while you develop an instinct about what looks right and what doesn't.

Again, it pays to buy from a reputable source and have expensive stamps expertized.

Faults. As mentioned, keep an eye open for faults, especially those that are not obvious such as thins, creases, pinholes, tears, and surface scrapes, which are often expertly colored over but visible under magnification. Dip stamps in watermark fluid to check for imperfections. Observe the courtesy of asking before dipping a stamp. Some dealers use lighter fluid to dip stamps, but it tends to leave an oily residue. Those who use lighter fluid deny this, but my own experimentation with dipping blank pieces of white paper has shown that after several dippings, the paper is no longer as white as the sheet from which it was cut. To be safe, use commercially prepared watermark fluid. Sometimes a fault becomes visible just at the moment the last bit of fluid flashes dry, so you may want to dip the stamp several times, holding it a various angles to the light as it dries.

Faults are sometimes hidden under hinges. Never remove a hinge without permission. Better yet, have the dealer remove it. If he won't, don't buy the stamp. Dealers often refuse to remove hinges that are heavily stuck down for fear of either damaging a stamp or revealing earlier damage. They feel it's more prudent to leave well enough alone and sell the stamp as is.

In the early 1970s I witnessed an episode at a fellow dealer's store that drives home the point about not removing hinges without permission. Two businessmen had met at the store to consummate the sale of a set of Zeppelins that one of them owned. By agreement, the dealer would be entitled to a ten-percent commission for arranging the meeting. The potential buyer lifted the Zepps with his tongs one by one and looked them over. The set was hinged, the hinges still in place.

Then the buyer pulled the hinge off the $2.60 value. As the hinge came off, it thinned the stamp. A loud and angry exchange followed. Voices thundered, faces reddened. It looked like they might come to blows.

Clearly the buyer was at fault. He should never have pulled the hinge off. The argument escalated from the seller insisting that the buyer buy the stamps at the undamaged price, to the seller finally refusing to sell the stamps at any price to a such a gosh-darn, irresponsible, ignorant fool (I've toned down the language considerably).

In the end, the seller kept the stamps and the buyer stalked out. I got the impression that he kept them because it gave him the right to bad-mouth the buyer in local collecting circles, which he did at every opportunity. The moral is, don't do anything that might damage a stamp that belongs to someone else.

Stamps can be rebacked to eliminate thins and pinholes. I've seen some beautiful examples of classic stamps expertly rebacked. They looked perfect, and that was the giveaway. Experienced dealers learn to be suspicious of any classic stamp that looks too good to be true. So should you.

An honorable dealer (and most are) will point out defects. If you think you've spotted a defect, don't allow yourself to be talked out of it. Follow your instinct. After all, you're the one who's going to have to explain it to the next buyer—the seller will be long gone. And let me assure you that if a dealer doesn't like the looks of something, he'll discount his offer heavily. Likewise, auctions scrupulously note every defect or anything that might possibly be construed as a defect because they don't want lots returned for being inaccurately described.

Dealers *always* put a magnifying glass (a ten-power loupe works well and can be carried in one's pocket) to an expensive stamp before buying. You should get into the same habit. And don't worry about offending a dealer by checking his stamps. He's used to seeing prudent buyers checking things out, and if he isn't, he sure as heck hasn't been around long.

Most of the problems mentioned in the foregoing paragraphs are surprisingly obvious if one just takes the time to look for them.

Expertizing. Expertizing offers peace of mind at modest cost. Knowledgeable buyers have stamps expertized to verify genuineness, confirm a valuable variety, and to report any faults, repairs, tampering, or deceptive alterations such as regumming, reperforating or removal of a cancellation to simulate an unused stamp. The two oldest and most respected expertizing services in the United States are the Philatelic Foundation (PF) and the American Philatelic Expertizing Service (APEX). Both rely on a multiple experts to examine submissions and render opinions.

Both services issue photographic certificates that illustrate subject stamps with perfect fidelity. And since no two stamps are identical—by virtue of margins, perforations and centering—the photographs serve as the philatelic equivalent of a fingerprint.

Some services indelibly mark stamps they consider to be fakes or frauds; however neither the Philatelic Foundation nor the American Philatelic Expertizing Service does. Avoid using any service that indelibly marks stamps because on occasion, an opinion is wrong and stamps thus marked are ruined. Both of the foregoing services stress that opinions rendered are just that—opinions. However, their opinions are rarely incorrect and their certificates are universally accepted as *bona fides* for stamps.

Both services maintain extensive reference collections of stamps, varieties, overprints, covers, and postal markings so that submissions can be compared with authentic examples and known fakes. Both services own sophisticated diagnostic equipment that can reveal almost any sign of tampering. And the expert committees of both services consist of some of the most experienced and widely respected authorities in philately.

Other expertizing services exist. Many are affiliated with stamp societies (such the American First Day Cover Society) and issue opinions on items within their specialty. In many foreign countries, expertizing is performed by recognized individual experts rather than by a panel of experts. While the practice is widely accepted abroad, collectors in this country feel more comfortable with the consensus approach.

Expertizing fees are based on a percentage of catalogue value, with a minimum fee applicable for items returned as not genuine. Obtain a submittal form before sending stamps for expert certificate. *Refer to the* Resource Guide.

One final word of caution. In some cases, unscrupulous parties have added information to or tried to remove information from a genuine certificate to enhance the description of a stamp. Recent certificates are almost foolproof; still it pays to be prudent. Most buyers prefer to have stamps on certificates older than ten years resubmitted for a new certificate. So, examine certificates, especially earlier ones, to make sure they have not been tampered with.

CAVEATS

Sad to say, the stamp trade, like other trades, is afflicted with schemes that offer the unwary almost no chance of making money and usually end up costing them money. Too often the phrase "rare stamp investment" is used as a marketing ploy to sell stamps. Those utilizing it are more interested in making themselves money than making investors money. So let's examine how not to invest.

The most noxious of these are telemarketing schemes, many of which develop leads through radio infomercials broadcast under the guise of investment shows. The pre-recorded infomercials are usually presented in interview format, often with the interviewer sounding more excited than the interviewee, no doubt because promoters know that listeners identify more closely with a neutral party than with one pitching a product. The interviewee usually cites puffed-up credentials (in most cases he is actually unknown in the philatelic trade) and exaggerated claims of investment performance. During the course of the presentation, listeners are enticed to call a toll-free number for further information and in some cases a free gift.

One telemarketer even created its own stamp index, which it called the Dow Jones Industrial Average of the stamp world. No one in the philatelic community had ever heard of it. It contained 36 stamps, which were not identified and which almost certainly were selected to show the most explosive gains. It would be like taking the 36 best performing stocks and making an index of them to portray stock market potential. It would give a grossly exaggerated picture of stock performance.

The telemarketer sent listeners slick brochures loaded with impressive charts and figures, including one that showed stamps appreciating nearly 40 percent during the previous 14 years. This astounding statistic was arrived at by averaging price performance from 1975 through 1989. It did not reflect that prices had fallen after 1980, that they had flattened out and only just begun to recover. Instead, it lumped the enormous run-up of prices during the 1975-1980 bubble with the later lackluster years, which gave a distorted view of the real situation. The Data Research Report also claimed that stamps had outperformed inflation by 150 to 200 percent per year during the previous hundred years!

The Data Research Report was laced with phrases such as stamps are "one of the best kept secrets in the investment world," and buzz words such as "blue chips" and "degrees of risk," all intended to mimic Wall Street language. It advised investing in the "bluest of the blue chip stamps." Among the items touted were stamps from Arab Emirates (most of which were held in low esteem in the philatelic community) and privately printed labels misrepresented as stamps.

In the early 1990s, another radio telemarketer bought impaired copies of high-catalogue stamps, such as the $1-$5 Columbian commemoratives of 1893, for a fraction of catalogue value, then resold them to investors at full catalogue or more. The markups amounted to five to ten times cost. The pitch was that the stamps were destined to skyrocket in value in 1992 because collectors would suddenly stampede to own them during the 500th anniversary of Columbus' landing. The problem was that the stamps were expensive to begin with, so expensive that few collectors would suddenly be motivated to rush out and plop down anywhere from $1,000 or $5,000 just because the anniversary had arrived. In reality, the anniversary year came and went with virtually no impact on the price of Columbians. But at the time, the pitch sounded plausible, especially to the unsophisticated.

Listeners who called got to talk to "account executives" who were, in reality, nothing more than pitchmen who filled their ears with golden words and happy talk about how touted issues would rise in value several times during the following four or five months. The "account executives" soft-peddled the pitch with a lot of flummery intended to sound like sophistication until they got a sense of just how much the traffic would bear, then closed with a hard sell. The "account executives" were skilled boiler-room pitchmen, not stamp experts. There were no set prices for stamps. Unlucky buyers paid as much for stamps as pitchmen sensed they could extract.

According to the pitch, buyers paid no commission; sellers paid a ten-percent commission. And selling sounded easy. Simply contact your "account executive" and advise him at what price to sell. A trade confirmation and a check would be sent, again within five business days of the transaction. It sounded very simple, very professional, but sellers found it nearly impossible to sell. "Account executives" chided them for being in a hurry, advised them to hold out for the big profits that always lay just around the corner.

The sales brochure contained the disclaimer that the investment service reserved the right to "make a market in selected issues" and "purchase stamps for its own account," phrases almost certainly intended to make the service sound large and sophisticated. In reality, it meant nothing, since it was virtually impossible to sell purchases back.

Both operations were shut down by the Federal Trade Commission within a short time after they began operating. The FTC complaint alleged that "investors" paid anywhere from two to ten times general retail prices.

The FTC recently (July 1997) shut down two more infomercial/telemarketing firms for fraudulent investment schemes, the most outrageous of which sold slightly misperforated U.S. stamps worth $5 to $10 each for prices ranging from $500 to $1,000 each. They sold the stamps as "very safe," and "very easy to convert into cash." Be suspicious of buying any investment through an infomercial.

During the 1980s, stamp bartering came into vogue. The barters typically consisted of trades of expensive stamps for real estate, yachts, and other high-dollar properties. Those offering stamps usually bought low-grade material (known as "seconds" or "space fillers") at auction for a fraction of catalogue value, then offered it in trade, citing catalogue value as a basis. The bartered stamps were usually expertized (remember most expertizers certify genuineness, *not condition*).

A surprising number of trades were consummated, often with the property owner exaggerating the value of his property too, so that in effect each side was trying to hoodwink the other. One of the biggest barter promoters was sued for trading stamps cataloguing $315,000 for a 14-acre, two-home lot. The recipient of the stamps tried to sell them, only to discover they were worth about $70,000-$75,000 on the market. The stamp man countered that the house appraised at $125,000 instead of $315,000 and sat on swampy ground. The case was eventually settled out of court.

At the time, the owner of some Colorado mountain property contacted me to do an appraisal on a million dollars worth of stamps that he'd been offered in trade for fifty acres of mountain land. I warned him that the stamps were defective and worth only about ten percent of the catalogue. I thought he'd be shocked, but instead he laughed. The property was quite remote, he said and maybe not out of line with the value of the stamps. And at that moment, I recalled hearing about some parcels of land that had sold for only a few dollars an acre because they were mostly on the sides of mountains and the cost of bringing roads and utilities in amounted to tens of thousands of dollars. I don't know who got the best of that deal.

At the time bartering was popular, the prices of remainders at auction rose from the historical level of five to ten percent of catalogue to as much as fifteen percent, on the strength of promoters buying material.

No account of stamp schemes would be complete without the notorious "Face on Mars" stamp. In 1989, Sierra Leone saluted the exploration of Mars with a set of 36 stamps and a souvenir sheet that depicted the well-known "Face on Mars," which is a mile-wide topographical feature resembling a human face. New-age folklore held that the face was carved by ancient astronauts and that similar faces exist elsewhere in the solar system, on the moon and even hidden under the Antarctica ice cap.

Shortly after the set was issued, an American promoter bought up nearly the entire supply for about $40 per set and began touting them in his newsletter as having tremendous appreciation potential—thousand of dollars. "Destined to be a bombshell" is the way he described the set. "Could well become one of the most valuable sets of stamps ever issued." Investors could buy sets for $100 each.

To support his claim, the promoter used a "space consultant" (with a long list of credentials) who made no secret that he possessed no philatelic knowledge or background upon which to base his opinion of value other than he felt the Face on Mars was "nothing less than the greatest discovery in the world." In his opinion, the value of the stamps depended on the intrinsic value of the event being commemorated. And since the Face on Mars was the greatest discovery in the world, the Sierra Leone sets were bound to be the most popular and sought after set of stamps in the world—worth $10,000 to $25,000 each. Philatelists who read these assertions must have thought the man out of touch with reality. No new issue from a small third-world nation such as Sierra Leone could ever be worth as much as $10,000.

The promoter said that buyers need not know anything about stamps to profit from the set. They need only sell them to someone else for more than they paid.

So, investors bought the sets and placed ads in classified sections of newspapers all over the country asking a variety of prices anywhere from a few hundred dollars to many thousands—and got takers! They wrote glowing letters to the promoter raving about their success. He published the testimonials in his newsletter, which only increased demand for the sheets.

"I sold my set for $6,000!" one writer gloated. "I sold a set for $5,000," another reported. "I should have bought more!" "I got $600!" "I moved a set for $2,000!" "Your advice is fantastic!"

Some of these entrepreneurs offered sets for as much as $15,000 to $20,000. Some claimed that the stamps were escalating at the rate of 200 percent *daily!* Some ads offered to trade the sheets for cars or trucks.

The more entrepreneurial among them even touted the sheets by direct mail to anyone they thought might be interested. Reproduced below is one such unsolicited letter received by us in June 1993. It speaks for itself.

I am interested in selling (2) Sierra Leone, "Face on Mars" stamp sets. This is a 1990 issue commerating [sic] space exploration. Only 5,000 sets were printed. There are 4 sheets of 9 stamps each, and a cover stamp [the souvenir sheet] showing the "Face on Mars" which was photographed by one of our spacecraft some 10 years ago. I have verification that these sets are selling for $5,000 each in several locations in the U.S. I have an ad in a Washington, D.C. paper. In the first week I received an offer of $2,500 for one set. My asking price is $5,000.

The issue price as approximately $100. I have seen ads asking $6,500 and as much as $10,000 per set! The value will likely increase in the fall of '93 and into the early months of '94. The reason???? In Oct. of '92 another spacecraft was launched whose purpose is to photograph the surface of Mars. It's camera has a resolution of 50 greater than the previous photos taken 10 years ago. Due to pressure from people who are interested in the "face," NASA has made assurances that the "face" and the nearby pyramidal shaped structures will definitely be photographed. The craft will reach Mars in Sept. of '93. The reason the stamp sets have escalated so greatly is the strong possibility that the face and other structures are not freaks of nature or geology, but were evidently built by intelligent beings. If you are interested in the purchases of one or more of the sets, please call.

The Face on Mars may have been built by intelligent beings, but those who paid inflated prices for the Face on Mars set were not of the same order of intelligence.

At the time all this was going on, the Face on Mars set could be had for about $75 in the philatelic trade. One investor called me to ask if I thought $7,500 was a fair price for the set. When I told him that the going rate was $75, he replied that I must out of touch with the market. He had paid $5,000 for his set and intended to advertise it in the newspaper for $7,500. Wasn't I aware of this, he demanded sarcastically. I was, I sighed, but also aware that one could buy all one wanted for $75. I even offered to fax him a copy of a retail ad from one of the philatelic weeklies, but he'd have none of it. Put off by his attitude, I decided to warn him that now that he knew the real market value of the set, he might be exposing himself to a suit for fraud if he sold one to someone for $7,500.

The moment I finished talking, he read me the riot act. Obviously, I was knocking the set because I didn't have any and was missing out on the profits. Then he hung up on me.

Another investment service offered high-catalogue stamps in mixed condition (within the trade "mixed" is a polite euphemism for damaged or impaired), selected specifically for their "investment rarity and high appreciation potential" at a discount of ten percent off catalogue value and guaranteed to buy them back at full catalogue (i.e. full catalogue at the time of original purchase) value but only on the tenth anniversary of the date of original purchase. It seemed like a no-lose proposition. At least the proposition claimed it was impossible to lose money, except that what kind of a return is an eleven-percent gain over ten years? Not very good. Perhaps the idea was that the stamps would rise in catalogue value and be worth more than the buy-back price—the buy-back acting as a safety net. The problem is that stamps in mixed condition rarely sell for more than 20 percent of catalogue. The purchase price of 90 percent of catalogue is highly inflated. The odds of the stamps rising enough to be worth more than the buy-back seem slim. On the tenth anniversary of purchase, investors are likely to find that the buy-back of full catalogue is the best price, and their eleven-percent return, pretty paltry.

It's all perfectly legal—and clever. In effect, the promoter buys stamps at, say, 20 percent of catalogue, sells them at 90 percent of catalogue, and has the use of investors' money for ten years at a cost of about one percent per year. What do investors get out it? A long shot that their portfolio might rise above cost, backed up by a guarantee of getting their original purchase price plus eleven percent back, which doesn't even come close to offsetting inflation. In effect, the buy-back price represents a net loss in purchasing power (yield minus inflation).

Keep your eyes open for red flags whether an investment offer comes in the form a direct mail piece, an infomercial, an investment seminar, or a telephone solicitation.

Red flags include: unsolicited calls; high pressure sales tactics; refusal to take no for an answer; a retort to every objection or question; unclear or evasive answers to questions; the promise of unrealistically high returns, especially in a short period of time; exaggerated claims of historical performance; guaranteed rates of return; guaranteed buy-backs; investments touted as sure things; inside information or special situations (often far-fetched but oddly plausible); pressure to buy quickly; pressure that only a few remain; pooh-poohing risk factors; puffed up credentials and fancy titles.

Speaking of guarantees, the most ridiculous one I ever encountered went something like this, "If you keep the stamps for at least five years, I guarantee a profit under normal circumstances, unless the country is in a recession or something like that, then all investments are subject to loss."

The whole idea of a guarantee is protect the buyer from loss. Without protection from downside risk, what good is a guarantee? By the way, the fellow offering the guarantee lasted only a couple of years, after which his buy-back became moot. Stay away from this kind of foolishness.

Stamp investment seminars are sometimes held in upscale hotel settings, complete with visual aids, refreshments, and high pressure sales techniques. The moment someone tries to twist your arm, walk away. And don't worry about offending high pressure pitchmen. Just say "no." It's better for you have the money and them be annoyed, than for them to have the money and you be annoyed.

In general, if something sounds too good to be true, it probably is. Use common sense. Consider investments carefully. Ask yourself, "If this possesses so much potential, why aren't the pitchmen buying it?"   Never allow yourself to be talked into buying stamps or any investment on the spur of the moment. Anything worth buying is worth thinking over.

In general, beware mass-marketed items and high pressure sales techniques.

The harder the pitch, the less likely the offer has merit.

Always make sure there's a secondary market for any investment you purchase. If there isn't, forget it.

Be cautious, be skeptical. Always remember the advice first cited in Latin thousands of years ago, *"caveat emptor"* (let the buyer beware).

Know your dealer or source.

SUMMARY

Successful stamp investing is a matter of knowledge and timing. A matter of planning what to acquire, when and how to acquire it, and when and how to sell it. The better you do your homework, the better your chance of success.

When considering a stamp for investment, you must ask yourself, "What about this stamp will cause it to increase in price?"

Arriving at the answer is like solving a puzzle. It requires homework and thought.

I know some stock investors whose success is directly attributable to the way in which they do their homework. They don't rely on brokers' advice. They select companies that appear to have promise and research them. They go into the field and examine the product or service. They pay attention to how the company treats it customers, its management philosophy, debt load, and financial performance. They pay attention to articles about them in the general press. Some even attend stockholders' meetings and board meetings or try to talk with management. They gather as much information as they can. Then they look at the price of the stock and try to decide if it's reasonable or already inflated by market expectations. They do their own research and call their own shots.

That's what I'm suggesting you do in stamps. Pursue knowledge relentlessly. Gather information relentlessly. Talk to dealers. Pay attention to what they're low on. Pay attention to buy advertisements, to which stamps seem to be in demand. Pay attention to retail prices. Attend stamp shows. Talk to collectors. Talk to postal clerks. Find out what people like and why. Find out what they're buying and what they're not. Visit philatelic libraries. Visit public libraries and university libraries for anything available on stamps. Read books and periodicals. Study catalogues. Join philatelic societies; membership fees are cheap compared to benefits received. Master the basics so well that decisions begin to come intuitively. Be your own tipster and play your cards close to the vest.

Pay keen attention to what is in demand and what is likely to be in demand in the future. As we have learned, demand is the key to price appreciation.

Let's summarize what we've learned:

- Invest in stamps only if you enjoy them.
- Identify your objective.
- Understand the nature of stamps and the stamp market. Remember that demand is the key to appreciation.
- Understand the nature of the underlying economy.
- Do your own homework. Strive for knowledge, be informed. A strategy is only as sound as its premise.
- Call your own shots. Never shift responsibility for making investment decisions to a third party. It's your money at risk, not the third party's. If your investment goes sour, they have nothing to lose.
- Be disciplined in your approach. Successful strategies require patience. Never let emotion sway you.
- Strive to be neither optimistic nor pessimistic, but realistic.
- Pay attention to timing. Buy and sell when the timing is right.
- Holding forever isn't a strategy. Profits don't occur until sales are made.
- Be patient. Look for buying opportunities. Scout selling outlets in advance.
- Don't buy on impulse. Decide in advance what you want and how much you ought to pay.

- Comparison shop.
- Never chase a hot market.
- Buy right. Above all, buying right is the key to profit. Avoid fully priced items except where underpriced by the market.
- Look for undervalued items.
- Pay attention to seasonal buying opportunities.
- Pay attention to the kind of items that dealers are eager to buy.
- Specialize, but don't choose an area that overreaches your budget. Remember that the sum of a specialized collection is often greater than the sum of its parts.
- Pay attention to trends. Figure out what the market wants and get there ahead of it.
- Be selective. Buy quality, both in terms of condition and in terms of investment potential. Concentrate on scarcity—real scarcity, not relative scarcity. Truly rare items and thinly spread items are not as vulnerable to market downturns as other items.
- When bidding at auction, determine your bidding limits in advance.
- View lots if possible.
- If you miss an opportunity, remember, there will always be another.
- Ask questions, think things over, then—and only then—make a decision.
- Sell into a rising market.
- Cold weather months are often the best months to sell.
- Sell intact if a grouping contains less desirable items.
- Avoid mass-marketed investment offers.
- Avoid stamps sold as investments through radio and television infomercials, high-pressure investment seminars, and telephone solicitations.
- Avoid new issues as investments. Some have speculative potential, but not many.

- If you speculate, get in, ride the wave, then get out. Never be afraid to take a profit. Once a speculation runs its course, time dilutes any gains.

- If a speculation doesn't work out, let go. Move on. Tying up money in a losing proposition wastes its potential.

- Don't chase fads, unless you're in at the beginning, on the ground floor. Then sell into the rising market.

- Diversify. Avoid putting more than five percent of your portfolio in any one item. If you have too much at risk in a single item, you may get nervous and make a hasty or ill-advised decision.

- Concentrate on material that is thinly spread and doesn't overhang the market.

- Avoid excessive quantities of any one item. That doesn't mean you can't have a variety of items relating to the same specialty.

- Avoid items that can be concentrated in a few hands or in the hands of speculators. They are subject to manipulation.

- As a general rule, be conservative.

- Never invest more than you can afford to lose.

- Use only discretionary income for investments. If you're forced to sell, you no longer control timing—and timing is everything.

- As a general rule, avoid leverage unless you are highly experienced.

- Don't be afraid to ask a professional for advice. Remember that a dealer's opinion is only as good as his experience. Get as many opinions as possible and weigh them. Truth emerges from consensus.

- Avoid doing business with anyone whose operation looks marginal.

- Avoid dealing with anyone whose credentials you can't check.

- Unused stamps generally appreciate more rapidly than used stamps. Stamps on cover and rarities sometimes are exceptions.

- Key stamps and sets usually appreciate more rapidly than other stamps.

- Avoid faulty stamps.

- Always check for faults—first.

- Have expensive stamps expertized.

- Don't pay a never-hinged premium for faulty stamps or stamps in less than fine-to-very-fine condition.

- Analyze statistical information carefully. Past performance is no guarantee of future performance.

- Don't let temporary phenomena frighten you. Time has a way of working things out. Recessions are always followed by booms.

- Be strong. Have faith in your investments. If you're unsure of yourself or your stamps, you will make ill-advised decisions. Scared money never wins.

- Take things slow. Remember, anything worth doing, is worth doing well. Good luck.

GLOSSARY

backstamp: a postmark placed on the reverse of a cover to indicate its arrival date or time.

banknote: a term used to describe U.S. definitive stamps of the 1870s to early 1890s printed under contract to the Post Office Department by the American Bank Note Company, the National Bank Note Company and the Continental Bank Note Company.

bisect: a stamp cut in half (often diagonally) and used as one-half the face value of the uncut stamp.

blind perforations: incompletely or partially impressed perforations, often barely indented into the paper and giving stamps the appearance of being imperforate. Stamps with blind perforations are not considered imperforate errors.

block: four or more stamps arranged in a rectangle.

B-O-B: back of the book. Includes stamps such as postage dues, special deliveries, parcel posts, revenues, etc.—anything listed in the rear of a catalogue following definitives and commemoratives.

booklet pane: a small sheetlet of stamps bound between card-stock covers by staples, thread or glue. Also self-adhesive stamps sold in small panes that can be folded for carrying in purse or wallet.

bourse: a show (or section of a stamp exhibition) devoted to booths from which dealers sell their wares to the stamp-collecting public. Bourses are often held in conjunction with stamp exhibitions.

cachet: (ka-shay). A decorative illustration printed, drawn or rubber-stamped on a cover, usually in connection with the first day of issue of a new stamp or some other special event. Usually occupies the left side of the cover.

cancel: an obliterating mark applied to a stamp, thereby rendering it invalid for future use. Cancellations may be applied by handstamp, machine, or pen.

canceled to order (CTO): cancellations applied by governments, often to full sheets. CTO stamps are often sold by governments in bulk to packet makers, approval dealers, etc. CTO stamps are generally not as desirable as genuinely postally-used stamps.

catalogue: a reference work that lists, illustrates, and prices postage stamps. Stamp catalogues can be general or specialized.

catalogue number: a number assigned by catalogue publishers to identify each separate stamp listed in the catalogue. Stamps that appear outwardly the same but differ in perforation, watermark, etc. are each considered to be a distinct collectible variety. Each variety is assigned its own catalogue number, despite the fact that they share the same design. To avoid having to publish an illustration of the underlying design with each variety, catalogue publishers assign an identifying number (as distinct from a catalogue number) to each design and make reference to it with the individual catalogue listings. The identifying number usually appears to the right of the catalogue number in the listings.

centering: the position of a stamp's design in relation to the perforations or edges of a stamp. Well-centered stamps possess even margins all around.

cinderella: a general, all-encompassing term applied to any stamp-like item not valid for postage, such as exhibition labels, Christmas seals, and the like. Anything that looks like a postage stamp but is not.

classic: an early issue, usually nineteenth-century.

coil stamp: stamps issued in rolls. Coils contain straight-edges on two parallel sides.

commemorative: a special stamp issued to honor a specific event, personality, anniversary or occasion, typically on sale for only a limited time.

commercial cover: a cover used for business correspondence (although more recently any cover of a non-philatelic nature) without any philatelic intent, as opposed to one created for some philatelic purpose.

condition: the state of a stamp with respect to centering, freshness, color, cancellation, and any other characteristics that might bear on its physical appearance.

cover: a philatelic term for an envelope, almost always implying that it has gone through the mail.

cut square: a piece containing the postage imprint cut from postal stationery, usually to facilitate mounting in an album.

definitive: a stamp, usually part of a series, available over an extended time for use on everyday mail. Also known as a regular issue.

die cut: cuts impressed onto self-adhesive stamps to facilitate separation, analogous to perforations.

duck stamp: a waterfowl-hunting stamp.

EFO: errors, freaks and oddities. A term applied to stamps with random minor production irregularities such as misaligned perforations, shifted colors, printing offset on reverse, ink smears, etc. *See* major error.

essay: an unadopted stamp design, either an entire design not used or a design very similar to the issued design except for small modifications.

expert certificate: a certificate issued by an acknowledged expert or expertizing body attesting to the genuineness or non-genuineness of a stamp or cover.

exploded: refers to a booklet that has been dissembled into individual panes.

face value: a stamp's denomination.

fake: an outright forgery; also a stamp (or cover) that has been modified to improve its value or desirability with the intent of defrauding a buyer.

fault: any defect affecting the appearance or integrity of a stamp such as a tear, cut, crease, thin, scrape, scuff, stain, fold, pin-hole, etc.

favor cancel: a cancellation applied to a stamp or cover as a favor by a postal employee, often on an item that might not normally have been used on mail or have gone through the mail, or with a postmarking device not normally used for that issue.

first day cover (FDC): a cover—usually cacheted—postmarked on the first day a stamp is available for sale.

flat-plate press: a printing press that utilizes flat printing plates and prints paper one sheet at a time.

grill: a waffle-like pattern impressed into some nineteenth-century stamps to break their paper fibers and make them more receptive to postmarking ink. Used to prevent the removal of cancellations and re-use of stamps.

gum: the adhesive on the back of a stamp.

gutter: the space between two panes of stamps on a sheet.

hammer price: the price paid for a lot by the highest bidder at an auction, exclusive of the buyer's commission.

heavily hinged (HH): hinged with strong glue that has disturbed the gum or will disturb it when removed.

hinge: a small piece of paper or glassine used to attach a stamp to an album page.

imperforate: lacking perforations.

intaglio: a method of printing in which the design is engraved (recessed) into a metal plate. Ink fills the recesses and when printed forms small ridges, which can be detected by magnifying glass or by running a finger over the design and feeling the ridges.

invert: a stamp with an element of the design upside down in relation to the other elements of the design.

job lot: a mishmash consisting of just about anything, loose stamps, covers, albums pages, mixtures, mint sets, remainders, etc., often sold by the carton. Dealers often dispose of surplus, disorganized material in the form of job lots. Sometimes called a mystery lot.

key: the most expensive or most difficult stamp in a series, set or era.

kiloware: a mixture of stamps on paper sold by the pound or kilogram, hence the name.

laid paper: paper showing alternate light and dark parallel lines impressed during manufacture. The lines show when dipped in watermark fluid.

lightly hinged (LH): hinged so that the hinge mark is barely noticeable. Implies that the gum has not been disturbed.

line pair: a pair of coil stamps on which a line appears between the stamps. On engraved, rotary-press coil stamps, lines are created by ink that fills the space where the curved plates join and is then printed in the same fashion as ink from recesses in an intaglio stamp design.

local: a stamp issued or used in locality (as opposed to nationally), either by postal carriers or by private carriers.

major error: usually refers to a stamp with a major production error such as a stamp lacking perforations, a stamp with a design element inverted, a stamp with a color or colors completely omitted, or a stamp printed in the wrong color. Minor production irregularities are referred to as EFOs. *See* EFO.

manuscript cancel: handwritten cancellation.

margin: the area between the edge of the design and the edge of the stamp. Also the border around a pane of stamps.

maximum card: a postcard bearing the same illustration or design as the stamp affixed to it and cancelled with first day or commemorative cancellation.

meter: a stamp printed by a postage metering machine such as those made by the Pitney-Bowes Company.

mint: an unused stamp with full gum as issued by the post office.

mounts: clear plastic pouches or containers used to protect and affix stamps to album pages.

multiple: a group of two or more unseparated stamps, such as a block, pair, strip, or pane.

never hinged (NH): a stamp that has never been hinged.

new issue: newly issued stamps, often received by subscription either directly from a postal administration or from a stamp dealer.

off-center: a stamp on which the design is poorly centered in relation to the perforations.

off paper: used stamps that have been soaked off paper. Most often applied to mixtures, which are sold either "on paper" or "off paper."

on cover: a stamp attached to a cover.

on piece: a stamp attached to a piece of paper torn or cut from an envelope or wrapper.

original gum: gum applied to a stamp at the time of its manufacture.

overprint: printing applied to stamps after regular production, typically to denote a special purpose (such as airmail), commemorate something, or as a control measure, etc. Overprints that change the denomination of a stamp are called surcharges.

packet: typically a printed, window envelope containing an assortment of common stamps for the beginner or general collector.

packet material: common, inexpensive stamps.

pair: two unseparated stamps.

pane: a finished "sheet" of stamps as sold in post offices, as distinct from a press or production sheet, which usually contains multiple panes of stamps.

perforations: the series of holes punched between stamps to facilitate their separation. The size of the holes and spacing vary from issue to issue. Perforations are measured by a perforation gauge.

plate block: a block of stamps with the printing plate number(s) appearing on the selvage. The size of the block can vary from issue to issue.

PNC: plate number coil. A coil stamp on which a small printing plate number (or numbers) appears at the bottom. Stamps with plate numbers appear at regular intervals on a roll of stamps, typically—but not necessarily—every 12, 24 or 52 stamps.

postcard: a privately produced card without postage imprinted on it and usually containing a printed greeting or view on the reverse. Often called a viewcard.

postal card: a card with postage imprinted on it by the postal service.

postal stationery: stationery sold by a postal service usually, but not always, with imprinted postage. Postal stationery includes postal cards, stamped envelopes, aerogrammes (airletter sheets), etc.

postmark: an official marking (usually circular but can be any shape, or in manuscript, or more recently, sprayed-on dot-matrix style characters) applied to a piece of mail, most often indicating date and place of mailing. Postmarks are often used to cancel stamps.

private treaty: an arrangement in which as stamp dealer acts in the capacity of agent for a seller, receiving a commission for his services.

proof: a trial impression made from a die or plate before regular production in order to check engraving, color, etc.

provisional: a stamp issued prior to the issuance of regular stamps or to meet a temporary shortage of regular stamps.

regummed: a stamp that has had new gum applied to simulate original gum.

reperforated: a stamp that has had perforations added to a straight-edge or to a perforated edge that has been trimmed to improve centering.

revenue stamp: stamp used to evidence payment of a fee or tax, often affixed to the article so taxed.

rotary press: a printing press on which the plates are curved in the form of a cylinder to facilitate printing of a continuous web of paper.

roulette: a philatelic term referring to a series of small slits (as opposed to round holes as in perforations) applied between stamps to facilitate separation.

selvage: the marginal area surrounding a sheet or pane of stamps. Sometimes spelled selvedge.

semi-postal: a postage stamp for which only part of the purchase price applies toward postage; the balance is collected for some other purpose, often a charitable cause. Semi-postals are usually denominated by two figures, the first applying toward postage, the second toward the other purpose, i.e. 50c+20c.

set: two or more stamps sharing a similar theme, motif or appearance, usually commemoratives, usually issued at the same time, and usually, but not always, of different denominations.

se-tenant: two or more different stamp designs printed next to one another on the same pane, souvenir sheet, booklet or coil.

short set: an incomplete set of stamps, usually comprised of only the lower denominations.

sound: free of faults.

souvenir sheet: a sheet, usually small, containing one or more stamps, usually bearing a commemorative marginal inscription, and usually issued for a special event or occasion.

stampless cover: a cover without stamps on which postage has usually been evidenced by handwritten notation or by handstamp, such as "Paid."

straight edge: the imperforate edge of a stamp (usually situated at the edge of a pane) that would otherwise normally have been perforated.

strip: three or more unseparated stamps attached side-to-side or end-to end (as opposed to in block form). A roll of 100 stamps is actually a strip of 100.

surcharge: an overprint for the purpose of changing the denomination of a stamp.

tagging: a luminescent coating applied during printing. It is used to facilitate the facing and handling of mail by automated equipment. Usually invisible to the naked eye, it can be observed under ultraviolet light. Tagging may cover all or part of a stamp.

tied: a term used to indicate that a cancellation marks both stamp and cover proving the stamp was attached to the cover at the time of cancellation.

topical collecting: collecting by the topic appearing on the stamp, such as art, horses or flowers. Known as thematic collecting in Great Britain.

unused: a stamp that has not been cancelled.

used: a stamp that has been cancelled.

viewcard: *see* postcard.

wallpaper: common stamps with little individual value, especially brightly colored foreign pictorials. Typically issued with low face value and sold in bulk by developing countries to stamp packet makers.

watermark: a design impressed into paper during its manufacture, sometimes visible when held up to light, most often visible only when immersed in watermark fluid. Do not immerse stamps in water to detect a "watermark"; use only watermark fluid designed for that purpose.

watermark fluid: an inert liquid (that will not affect gum) used to detect watermarks. Several brands are commercially produced and available at stamp dealers.

wove paper: paper with a uniform texture showing no dark or light pattern when immersed in watermark fluid.

RESOURCE GUIDE

PHILATELIC PERIODICALS

American Philatelist (monthly). P.O. Box 8000, State College, PA 16803; (814) 237-3803. *Monthly journal of the American Philatelic Society.*

Global Stamp News (monthly). P.O. Box 97, Sidney, OH 45365; (937) 492-3183. *Bargain-priced subscription rate. Great for the beginner, intermediate, or advanced collector.*

Linn's Stamp News (weekly). P.O. Box 29, Sidney, OH 45365; (937) 498-0801; website: www.linns.com. *Excellent general paper covering all aspects of philately.*

Mekeel's and Stamps Magazine (weekly). P.O. Box 5050, White Plains, NY 10602; (800) 635-3351; fax: (914) 997-7261.

Scott Stamp Monthly. P.O. Box 828, Sidney, OH 45365; (937) 498-0802; website: www.scottonline.com. *Excellent publication with articles of interest to all levels.*

Stamp Collector (bi-monthly). 700 East State Street, Iola, WI 54990; (715) 445-2214; fax: (715) 445-4087; website: www.collectit.net.

CATALOGUES

Brookman United States, United Nations & Canada Stamps & Postal Collectibles. Brookman Stamp Company, 10 Chestnut Drive, Bedford, NH 03110. *Stamp price guide. Published annually.*

Catalogue of Errors on U.S. Postage Stamps. Krause Publications, 700 East State Street, Iola, WI 54990. *Catalogue of major errors on U.S. stamps. Published annually.*

Harris US/BNA Postage Stamp Catalog. H.E. Harris & Co., P.O. Box 817, Florence, AL 35631. *Catalogue/retail list for U.S. and British North America. Published annually.*

Krause-Minkus Standard Catalog of U.S. Stamps. Krause Publications, 700 East State Street, Iola, WI 54990. *Catalogue of U.S. postage stamps featuring a wealth of information about each issue. Published annually.*

Planty Photo Encyclopedia of Cacheted First Day Covers. Earl Planty. Michael A. Mellone, P.O. Box 206, Stewartsville, NJ 08886. *Highly detailed multi-volume catalogue on cacheted FDCs of the classic period, 1901-1939.*

Scott Standard Postage Stamp Catalogue. Scott Publishing Co., P.O. Box 828, Sidney, OH 45365. *Multi-volume set covering the world. Published annually.*

Scott U.S. First Day Cover Catalogue and Checklist. Mike Mellone. Scott Publishing Co., P.O. Box 828, Sidney, OH 45365. *Detailed listings for U.S. first day covers. Published annually.*

Scott Specialized Catalogue of U.S. Stamps. Scott Publishing Co., P.O. Box 828, Sidney, OH 45365. *Comprehensive listing of all U.S. postage stamps. Published annually.*

The Postal Service Guide to U.S. Stamps. United States Postal Service, Box 419636, Kansas City, MO 64179-0996. *Noteworthy for its full-color illustrations.*

ELECTRONIC MEDIA

The Global Stamp Exchange. 6175 NW 153rd Street, Suite 201, Miami Lakes, FL 33014; website: www.stampfinder.com. *Online trading.*

Linn's Guide to Stamp Collecting Software. William F. Sharpe. Linn's Stamp News, P.O. Box 29 Sidney, OH 45365; website: www.linns.com. *Rates and evaluates software and stamp collecting sites on the Internet.*

GENERAL PHILATELIC READING

Basic Philately. Kenneth A. Wood. Krause Publications, 700 East State Street, Iola, WI 54990.

Facts and Fantasy About Philately. John M. Hotchner. P.O. Box 1125, Falls Church, VA 22041. *Delightful book of stamp collecting wit and wisdom by one of America's best-known philatelic writers.*

Fundamentals of Philately. L. N. Williams. American Philatelic Society, P.O. Box 8000, State College, PA 16803.

Linn's U.S. Stamp Yearbook. Linn's Stamp News, P.O. Box 29, Sidney, OH 45355. *Published annually, gives details regarding design, production, problems, etc., for each stamp issued that year.*

Nassau Street. Herman Herst, Jr. Amos Press, Inc., P.O. Box 29, Sidney, OH 45365. *Enjoyable memoir of a stamp dealer active during the golden era of philately. One of philately's best selling books.*

On The Road: The Quest for Stamps. Stephen R. Datz. General Philatelic Corporation, P.O. Box 402, Loveland, CO 80539. *Veteran dealer's true-life experiences buying stamp collections from the public all across America.*

Philatelic Forgers: Their Lives and Works. Varro E. Tyler. Linn's Stamp News, P.O. Box 29, Sidney, OH 45365.

Still More Stories to Collect Stamps By. Herman Herst, Jr. Mekeel's Stamp News, P.O. Box 5050, White Plains, NY 10602. *More stories by the author of* Nassau Street.

The Wild Side: Philatelic Mischief, Murder, and Intrigue. Stephen R. Datz. General Philatelic Corporation, P.O. Box 402, Loveland, CO 80539. *A stamp dealer's first-hand experiences with a rogue's gallery of scoundrels, eccentrics, and misfits.*

The World's Greatest Stamp Collectors. Stanley M. Bierman. Linn's Stamp News, P.O. Box 29, Sidney, OH 45365. *Highly readable biographies of the world's greatest stamp collectors.*

REFERENCE GUIDES

American Stamp Dealers Association Membership Guide. American Stamp Dealers Association, 3 School St., Glen Cove, NY 11452-2548. *Cross referenced by specialty.*

The Buyer's Guide to Selected U.S. Postage Stamps. Stephen R. Datz. General Philatelic Corporation, P.O. Box 402, Loveland, CO 80539. *Detailed stamp-by-stamp analysis of quality U.S. stamps for the selective buyer, including premium characteristics, gum and hinging, fakes and problem stamps, when to expertize, etc. Completely illustrated.*

How to Detect Damaged, Altered, and Repaired Stamps. Paul W. Schmid. Krause Publications, 700 East State Street, Iola, WI 54990. *The most authoritative and easy-to-use book on the subject of altered U.S. stamps. Well illustrated. Highly recommended.*

Micarelli Identification Guide to U.S. Stamps. Charles Micarelli. Scott Publishing Co., P.O. Box 828, Sidney, OH 45365. *Comprehensive identification guide to U.S. definitive stamps, fully illustrated, and especially useful for hard-to-identify nineteenth-century issues.*

StampFinders Stamp Selection Guides. USID, Inc., 6175 N.W. 153rd St. Suite 221, Miami Lakes, FL 33014. *Investment-oriented stamp price performance guides.*

This is Philately; An Encyclopedia of Stamp Collecting. Kenneth A. Wood. Krause Publications, 700 East State Street, Iola, WI 54990.

Top Dollar Paid: The Complete Guide to Selling Your Stamps. Stephen R. Datz. General Philatelic Corporation, P.O. Box 402, Loveland, CO 80539. *Best-selling how-to guide loaded with practical information and entertaining narrative about the stamp trade. Not only for sellers, but for all who buy or collect stamps.*

DEALERS' ORGANIZATIONS

American Stamp Dealers Association (ASDA). 3 School Street, Suite 205, Glen Cove, NY 11542-2548; (516) 759-7000; fax: (516) 759-7014; website: website: www.amerstampdlrs.com.

American Philatelic Society (APS). P.O. Box 8000, State College, PA 16803; (814) 237-3803; fax: (814) 237-6128; website: www.west.net/~stamps1/aps.html.

STAMP SOCIETIES

American Philatelic Society (APS). P.O. Box 8000, State College, PA 16803; (814) 237-3803; fax: (814) 237-6128; website: www.west.net/~stamps1/aps.html.

STAMP INSURANCE

American Philatelic Society Insurance Program. P.O. Box 8000, State College, PA 16803; (814) 237-3803; fax: (814) 237-6128.

Collectibles Insurance Agency. P.O. Box 1200, Westminster, MD 21158; (888) 837-9537; fax: (410) 876-9233; website: www.collectinsure.com.

EXPERTIZING

American Philatelic Expertizing Service. P.O. Box 8000, State College, PA 16803; (814) 237-3803. *Send for submission forms before submitting stamps.*

Philatelic Foundation. 70 West 40th Street, 15th Floor, New York, NY 10018; (212) 221-6555. *Send for submission forms before submitting stamps.*

MUSEUMS

Hall of Stamps. United States Postal Service, 475 L'Enfant Plaza, Washington, DC 20260.

National Postal Museum. Smithsonian Institution, 2 Massachusetts Avenue, NE, Washington, DC 20560.

Spellman Museum of Stamps and Postal History. 235 Wellsley Street, Weston, MA 02193; (781) 768-8367.

PHILATELIC LIBRARIES

American Philatelic Research Library (APRL). 100 Oakwood Avenue, State College, PA 16803; (814) 237-3803; fax: (814) 237-6128. *One of the largest collections of philatelic books in the world. Open to the public; borrowing by members only.*

The Collectors Club. 22 East 35th Street, New York, NY 10016; (212) 638-0559; fax: (212) 481-1269. *Open to the public; borrowing by members only.*

The Postal History Foundation. 920 North First Avenue, Tucson, AZ 85719; (520) 623-6652.

Rocky Mountain Philatelic Library. 2038 South Pontiac Way, Denver, CO 80224; (303) 759-9921.

San Diego County Philatelic Library. 4133 Poplar Street, San Diego, CA 92105.

Wineburgh Philatelic Research Library. University of Texas at Dallas, P.O. Box 830643, Richardson, TX 75083.

GIFTING (Non-profit)

Stamps for the Wounded. P.O. Box 1125, Falls Church, VA 22041.

APPENDIX

The following is reproduced with permission of the American Stamp Dealers Association.

The Stamp Dealer's Obligations and Responsibilities When Selling Stamps as an Investment

This pamphlet is published as a public service by the ASDA as a guide to those who might desire information on investing in philatelic properties. While every effort has been made to be thorough and informative, no claim is made for its completeness or accuracy, and no present or future liability shall be incurred by the ASDA as a result of publishing and/or distributing this pamphlet.

It is the sole responsibility of each investor to make his or her own decisions, and this pamphlet is designed to inform and aid such investors to make such decisions.

It is the stamp dealer's obligation to provide as much pertinent information as possible to the prospective investor. This information should be current and include the dealer's qualifications, the role of stamps in meeting the investor's goals, risks of philatelic investing, the purchase, storage, and disposition of philatelic material and other pertinent data.

Qualifications To Sell Stamps As An Investment Or To Act In the Capacity Of a Stamp Investment Counsellor

The stamp dealer should provide to all prospective investors information indicating his or her qualifications.

The investor should ask for the following information:

A. Investment knowledge.

    1. Courses related in Economics, Investments, Finance, and Accounting.

    2. Experience related in Economics, Investments, Finance, and Accounting.

B. Philatelic Experience.

    1. Dealer, part-time? Full-time? Firms? How long?

    2. Philatelic Society Memberships - (good reference to check).

        a. Dealer organizations - how many continuous years?

        b. Collector organizations - how man continuous years?

C. Business Status.

    1. Form of business you are dealing with: partnership, corporation, sole proprietor. Who are the principal parties from whom you are buying?

    2. Bank references.

    3. D & B report, if possible.

    4. A statement of licenses, bonds, and insurance (if you consign to a dealer).

D. Personal Background.

    1. Ever been convicted of a felony? Fraud?

    2. Ever filed for bankruptcy or Chapter Eleven?

    3. Ever been expelled from a philatelic society?

Determining The Goals And Aims of The Investor

The dealer has an obligation to an investor to help him or her achieve the goals they desire. Your investment goals should take the following into consideration.

A. Purpose and duration of the investment.

    1. Retirement.

    2. Children's education.

    3. Other.

    4. Time plan - three years, five years, twenty years.

B. Desired compound rate of return on investment.

C. Degree of soundness.

    1. Investment.

    2. Speculation.

D. Liquidity of Philatelic investments (national or international marketing).

E. Diversification of stamps as related to the overall investment program.

    1. What percentage of your total net worth?

    2. What percentage of new investment moneys?

F. Tax Treatment (Accountants' and Attorneys' advice should be sought).

    1. Income vs. Capital Gains.

    2. Corporate tax structures.

    3. IRA plans, Keogh plans, . . . etc.

    4. Estate taxes.

    5. Sales taxes or VAT (other countries).

G. Control of material.

    1. Individual.

    2. Corporate.

    3. Trust.

H. Timing of investments.

   1. Lump sum.

   2. Sporadic.

   3. Periodic.

Hazards and Risks

Philatelic prices are determined by supply and demand; they will go up and down with the demand to purchase items. The dealer has a responsibility to reveal and discuss with a prospective investor that there are various hazards and risks in philatelic investing. The following factors should be included in such a discussion.

A. Influence of time on risk, both short and long term.

B. Influence of the age of stamp on risk.

   1. Classic issues.

   2. Intermediate issues.

   3. New issues.

C. Stamp production.

   1. There are countries and firms that print stamps and covers which have little or no relationship to that nation's postal system. Many stamp issues are demonetized shortly after issue.

   2. There are fakes, forgeries and altered stamps in the marketplace.

D. Political and economic influences of the collecting country.

   1. Short or long term.

   2. National or international.

Investing

Investment in philatelic material requires decisions as to where to buy, quality, and what to invest in. It is the obligation of the dealer to educate and discuss with the prospective investor all these facets, including but not necessarily limited to the various considerations listed below.

What to Look for in Your Dealer

A. Does the dealer guarantee the items for description and authenticity?

B. Be aware that the dealer must make a profit to provide his services.

C. Ask the dealer questions. Let them teach you.

D. Don't expect a dealer to have all the answers. No one person knows everything in this business.

E. Communication between you and the dealer is very important. Let him know exactly what you want.

F. Learn the roles of the collector, investor, and the dealer in the philatelic marketplace.

G. Most stamp dealers are not considered experts in legal and tax matters. Investors should seek advice of their own accountants and attorneys on specific arrangements.

A. Things you should know about what you are investing in.

   1. How many of an item were printed, what is the ease of availability and salability?

   2. What do they catalog for, sell for, or postal value?

   3. Recommendations of what items to purchase are subjective. Is this what you want?

   4. Is there a demand for this country of issue. Are there future buyers?

B. Philatelic Investment Fields.

   1. Commemoratives, definitives, semi-postals, and airmail stamps.

   2. "Back of the book" stamps (revenues, tax, documentary, permit stamps, etc.).

   3. Postal history and covers.

   4. Proofs and essays.

   5. Errors.

C. Philatelic areas.

    1. Country or regional.

    2. Topical.

    3. Specialized area within a country or topic.

D. Types of investment stamps.

    1. Individual rarities.

    2. Medium priced stamps in limited quantities.

    3. Less expensive stamps in large quantities.

    4. Build a one-of-a-kind fine collection in a chosen area.

    5. Manipulation-possibility of obtaining market control of an item.

E. Diversification.

    1. Well balanced portfolio.

    2. Need for periodic review.

F. Condition criteria, quality desired for investment purposes. Prices vary according to these criteria.

    1. Centering.

    2. Freshness.

    3. Blemishes.

    4. Damage.

    5. Altered.

G. Sources to obtain stamps.

    1. Auction sales (read terms of sale).

    2. Private treaty.

    3. Dealers stock.

    4. Other collectors (all sales probably final, no recourse).

H. Fees.

    1. An arrangement on consultation fees should be agreed upon prior to seeking detailed investment advice.

2. When there are brokerage or agent fees for the purchase of material for the investor's account, these should be agreed upon prior to the initial purchase of stamps as an investment.

3. Prior arrangement of consultation and/or brokerage fees should be made before including the stamp dealer in any testamentary instructions.

Maintenance of Philatelic Investment Properties

Proper care in preservation is necessary to reach investment objectives. This is the investor's responsibility with the help and advice of the dealer.

A. How to store material.

1. Mounts, stockbooks, albums, etc.

2. Private safes, bank vaults, etc.

3. Temperature and humidity control.

B. Insurance coverage and types.

1. Fire, casualty, and theft.

2. How and where to obtain philatelic insurance.

3. Term life insurance for prospective investors to guarantee completion of their goals. Disability income insurance for prospective investors to guarantee continuity of any planned regular period investments.

Disposition of Philatelic Investment Properties

The proper disposition of philatelic investments is just as important as the acquisition. The dealer has a responsibility to discuss the various methods and timing of such disposition with the advice and counsel of the client's accountants and attorneys.

A. Certificates - Currently it takes several months to get a certificate; therefore, it is suggested certificates should be obtained as soon as possible. This could speed up the sale and payment of your material.

B. Timing factor relative to goals and market forces.

1. Keep up with the market so you will have an idea what the current values are.

2. The dealer who sold you the stamps can usually help you decide an advantageous time to sell.

C. Methods of sale.

   1. Public auctions.

   2. Private treaty.

   3. Sale to dealer.

   4. Sale to collector.

D. Gift or gifts.

   1. To a relative.

   2. To a charity.

   3. Tax consequences.

E. Possible Estate Disposal.

   1. Will of prospective investor to include detailed provisions for disposition.

   2. Testamentary trusts.

   3. Estate tax ramifications of storage location.